Donor Motivations

Why People Give and How Fundraisers Can Earn Their Support

Dr. Bobby Olszewski

emerson

Management & Consulting Group, Inc.

Winter Garden, FL
© 2026

TABLE OF CONTENTS
PART 1
DONOR MOTIVATIONS RESEARCH INTRODUCTION

PART 2
QUANTITATIVE RESEARCH ANLAYSIS

PART 1: DONOR MOTIVATIONS RESEARCH INTRODUCTION

INTRODUCTION

THE AUTHOR'S PHILANTHROPIC JOURNEY

The first time Bobby Olszewski understood the power of giving, he wasn't a scholar, an elected official, or a nonprofit leader. He was a kid watching his parents work hard, serve their church, and step up whenever someone in the community needed help. He learned early that generosity wasn't measured in the size of a gift, but in the sincerity of it, in the desire to lift someone up, even if just for a moment. That early lesson never left him.

Growing up in Orlando, Bobby was drawn to two things that would later define his life: service and community. Both taught him discipline. Both taught him teamwork. But most importantly, both revealed how ordinary people can do extraordinary things when they believe in something bigger than themselves.

He didn't know it then, but those early influences would one day shape a career spent in public leadership, nonprofit advancement, sports development, and academic research on what motivates people to give.

A Path Forged Through Service

Bobby's journey into leadership did not begin with a campaign speech or a boardroom decision, it began with showing up. He served his community long before he held a title. Over the years, he found himself supporting causes that mattered deeply to him including Special Olympics Florida, Florida Citrus Sports, church programs, and local charities that helped families and children.

Eventually, community members asked him to take on more formal roles. That commitment led him to public office, first as a Winter Garden City Commissioner and later as a State Representative representing Orange County, Florida for a district including the Walt Disney World Resort, Universal Orlando Resort, Sea World, and the Orange County Convention Center. In both positions, he raised significant funds for community programs, nonprofits, athletic initiatives, local events, and charitable causes supporting children, veterans, families in crisis, and neighborhood projects. Public service, he discovered, was fundraising in its purest form, inspiring people to invest in the well-being of others.

A Heart for Nonprofits and Philanthropy

Bobby's work with the YMCA of Central Florida would become one of the most important chapters of his nonprofit life. Serving as Board Chair and two times as Fundraising Chair for the West Orange County community, he helped one of the largest

YMCA associations in the country, championing programs that strengthened families, supported youth, and anchored communities.

He listened to donors.
He learned from them.
He saw what moved them.

And after years of conversations with community supporters, athletes, CEOs, families, and first-time givers, he began asking deeper questions:

Why do people give?

What motivates generosity?

How do we inspire someone who has never heard of our mission before today?

Why do some donors give once while others give for a lifetime?

Those questions ultimately fueled his doctoral research.

A Researcher with a Fundraiser's Heart

Bobby pursued his Ph.D. in Business Administration to understand the human motivations behind giving. His dissertation focused on a unique environment, the Basilica of the National Shrine of Mary, Queen of the Universe within the Roman Catholic Diocese of Orlando in Florida. The Basilica serves tourists instead of parishioners, where every donor is typically a first-time donor with no previous relationship. It was, academically and practically, the perfect test case.

From nearly 500 surveyed donors, he studied what drives individuals to give when no relationship, no history, and no obligation exist. The findings were powerful, reshaping his understanding of nonprofit development and influencing the strategies he would later teach, lead, and write about.

Achievement.
Affiliation.
Philanthropy.
Power.

These motivations became the framework through which he understood generosity and the foundation for this book.

Sports as a Classroom for Leadership and Giving

Alongside his nonprofit and academic work, Bobby spent significant years working in the world of sports, not only as a communicator and strategist, but as a partnership builder and fundraiser. His experience with College Football Bowl games, the PGA Tour, the LPGA Tour, the AMA Motocross Series, and representing various professional athletes as a sports agent, gave him access to a different side of philanthropy. This experience was anchored in the corporate partnerships, sponsorships, charity events, and athlete-driven initiatives that define modern sports philanthropy.

He saw how athletes use their platform for good.

He saw how sports organizations raise millions for causes across the country.

He saw how generosity and competition can coexist, making the other stronger.

Those experiences taught him that fundraising isn't just about money. It's about meaning. It's about making a personal connection. It's about shared purpose.

A Voice for Leaders Who Want to Inspire Generosity

Today, Bobby unites all these chapters of his life, his public service, academic research, nonprofit leadership, sports sponsorship experience, communication background, and storytelling skill to help organizations inspire generosity with purpose and integrity. He is currently helping with the efforts to bring Major League Baseball to Orlando seeking to make a difference in the lives of children and families in his hometown community.

He believes philanthropy is deeply human.

He believes donors want to make a difference.

He believes nonprofits change the world one relationship at a time.

And he believes that when leaders understand why people give, they can unlock a level of generosity that transforms missions, strengthens communities, and changes lives.

This book is the culmination of that journey, a guide for every nonprofit professional, fundraiser, community leader, and board member who wants to build stronger relationships, inspire deeper generosity, and lead with heart.

CHAPTER 1: WHY DONORS GIVE AND WHY UNDERSTANDING MATTERS

Most nonprofit leaders can recall a moment that still doesn't make sense.

A donor who gave generously without being asked.

A carefully prepared proposal that went nowhere.

A small first-time gift that turned into lifelong support.

A longtime supporter who quietly drifted away.

These moments are not random.

They are not left to chance.

And they are not simply about income, timing, or tax strategy.

They are about motivation.

This book exists because too much modern fundraising focuses on *how* to ask and not enough time is spent understanding *why donors say yes in the first place.*

What the Nonprofit Field Gets Right and What It Often Misses

Nonprofit professionals are exceptionally skilled at managing the mechanics of fundraising.

We track giving history.

We segment lists.

We refine appeals.

We optimize campaigns.

We steward donors thoughtfully.

And yet, even the most experienced leaders will admit there is still a gap.

We often know **what** donors did.

We know **when** they gave.

We know **how much** they contributed.

But we rarely know **why**.

Without that understanding, fundraising becomes reactive.

With it, fundraising becomes intentional.

When Experience Meets Evidence

Years of leadership in nonprofit organizations, public service, and large-scale fundraising reveal patterns that every practitioner recognizes intuitively.

People give when something resonates.

They give when they feel moved.

They give when the mission aligns with something personal.

But intuition alone is not enough to build sustainable generosity.

That realization led to a deeper question:

Can donor motivation be studied, measured, and applied in a way that strengthens real-world fundraising?

This book answers that question with a clear yes.

A Research Environment That Mirrors Today's Fundraising Reality

The research behind this book did not take place in a controlled lab or among a cultivated donor list.

It took place in one of the most demanding environments imaginable for fundraisers:

A nonprofit with no regular donors.

No built-in donor base.

No membership model.

No expectation of repeat giving.

At the Basilica of the National Shrine of Mary, Queen of the Universe in Orlando,

Florida, nearly every donor is practically a first-time donor.

Visitors arrive with no prior relationship.

They are not solicited.

They are not cultivated.

They are not asked to commit.

And yet, they give.

That makes this environment uniquely valuable for nonprofit leaders.

Because it strips fundraising down to its core question:

What motivates generosity when no one has to give at all?

What the Research Revealed

Surveying hundreds of donors, this research identified four motivational drivers that

consistently influence giving behavior:

Achievement

Affiliation

Philanthropy

Power

These motivations are not labels.

They are lenses.

They explain why two donors can experience the same appeal and respond completely

differently.

They explain why data excites some donors while stories move others.

They explain why recognition inspires generosity in some cases and discourages it in others.

Most importantly, this specific research study revealed that **Achievement and Philanthropy** are the strongest predictors of giving among first-time donors.

That insight alone has profound implications for acquisition strategies, digital campaigns, events, and donor onboarding.

Why This Matters Now

The nonprofit sector is operating in a more challenging environment than at any time in recent memory.

Donor participation is declining.

Budgets are tighter.

Competition for attention is increasing.

First-time donor retention remains stubbornly low.

In this context, organizations cannot afford to guess.

They must understand what truly motivates generosity.

This book is not about replacing relationships with research.

It is about strengthening relationships through understanding.

What This Book Will Do for You

As you move through this book, you will gain:

• a practical framework for identifying donor motivation

• language that aligns with how donors actually think and feel

• tools for tailoring asks, stewardship, and campaigns

• insight into first-time donor behavior

• a method for turning intuition into strategy

You will not be asked to become a researcher.

You will be given research you can use and apply immediately.

The Shift This Book Invites

Fundraising does not fail because nonprofits lack passion.

It struggles when organizations misunderstand motivation.

When you understand why donors give, you stop trying to persuade.

You start aligning.

You stop chasing gifts.

You start inviting partnership.

And generosity becomes something donors want to repeat.

This chapter sets the foundation for everything that follows.

Because before we can change how we ask, we must understand why donors answer.

CHAPTER 2: DONOR MOTIVATIONS PRELUDE

A Moment, A Mission, A Gift: Why Donors Give Even When They Don't Have To

She stood in the back pew as if she were hiding from the world.

Her conference badge still hung around her neck.

Her shoulders curled with the weight of deadlines, family responsibilities, and decisions that refused to wait for the right moment.

She wasn't a parishioner.

She wasn't a donor.

She wasn't even sure why she followed the shuttle driver's suggestion to "stop by the Basilica if you have a minute."

She wasn't even Catholic, but when she stepped through the doors, the air changed.

It wasn't just the architecture, the artwork, and the serenity.

It wasn't just the music drifting through the sanctuary.

It was the feeling, a rare, almost sacred sense of being allowed to pause and breathe.

She prayed, though she hadn't planned to.

She let her mind go quiet for the first time in days.

And then something happened that development officers, nonprofit leaders, fundraisers, and board members spend entire careers trying to understand.

As she turned to leave, she noticed a modest offering box by the bronze doors.

Nothing flashy.

No one watching.

No steward asking.

Just a box.

She had no prior relationship with the Basilica of the National Shrine of Mary, Queen of the Universe before coming to her work conference in Orlando.

She didn't know its mission statement, its leadership, or its financial needs.

She certainly hadn't been cultivated, nurtured, or stewarded.

She simply felt something.

And in that feeling, she reached for her wallet.

She folded a bill.

Slipped it into the envelope after filling out her information on the cover.
Placed it inside the collection box.

She walked out with a sense of relief, lighter, somehow, than when she entered.

That moment happens thousands of times every year.

A stranger enters.

A heart opens.

A gift is given.

Not because someone asked.

Not because someone cultivated.

Not because someone explained impact metrics, recognition levels, or strategic priorities.

But because something inside them said:

"This mattered to me and I want to give something back."

For decades, fundraisers have been taught to focus on technique with the right ask, the right timing, the right channel, the right stewardship sequence.

But moments like this challenge that thinking.

They reveal a truth that every nonprofit professional needs to embrace:

People give long before they fully understand why.

Their motivation sparks the gift, not the strategy.

Generously. Consistently. Meaningfully.

For fundraisers, this isn't just interesting.

It's revolutionary.

Because if we can understand why strangers give, we can understand how to inspire anyone to give again and give more deeply.

This book explains the motivations that drive those moments, and how nonprofits can honor them, activate them, and build lasting relationships from them.

It begins with a simple question that changes everything:

What moves the human heart to give when the head has no prior reason to?

Understanding that answer may be the most important work in modern philanthropy.

CHAPTER 3: DONORS MOTIVATIONS FOREWORD

Understanding Donor Motivations: The Philanthropic Perspective of Why We Give

Nonprofit professionals spend countless hours refining campaigns, segmenting audiences, managing databases, and writing compelling appeals. Yet the most powerful force driving charitable behavior is something far more fundamental than strategy or timing. It is motivation.

Every act of giving, whether a spontaneous five-dollar gift or a transformational five hundred-thousand-dollar contribution, is rooted in an internal psychological trigger. Donors rarely articulate this trigger consciously. They simply act when something inside them says:

"This matters."

"This feels meaningful."

"This aligns with who I am."

Nonprofit fundraisers see the results of these internal motivations every day:

• Donors who give before asking a single question
• Donors who give again after years of silence
• Donors who give more when trust and clarity rise
• Donors who never give because motivation was never activated

Understanding donor motivation is no longer optional. It is the foundation of sustainable fundraising.

Why Motivation Is the Missing Variable in Fundraising Strategy

Most nonprofit organizations excel at tracking behavioral data such as:

• gift frequency
• average gift size
• campaign response rates
• seasonal patterns
• donor retention metrics

But very few measure the psychological data that drives those behaviors:

• Why did the donor give at all
• What internal need was fulfilled by giving
• Which motivation would inspire a second gift
• What meaning the donor attached to the act of giving

As a result, organizations often build fundraising campaigns based on observable actions instead of underlying motivations, causing lost revenue, inconsistent engagement, and weaker long-term loyalty.

This book fills that gap by translating rigorous academic research into practical strategies that fundraisers, nonprofit executives, and development teams can apply immediately.

A Unique Natural Laboratory for Studying Pure Motivation

This study centered on an uncommon nonprofit environment that allowed motivations to be measured with scientific accuracy:

A Catholic basilica serving tourists instead of parishioners.

Visitors often had:

• no prior connection to the organization,
• no long-term relationship with the institution,
• no external social pressure to give,
• and no expectation of reciprocity.

Yet many still made monetary contributions.

This created a rare research setting in which donation behavior occurred free from relationship-based bias, allowing the study to isolate the true motivational drivers that inspire first-time donors, exactly the group most nonprofits struggle to cultivate.
For fundraisers, this has direct relevance:

If you can understand why a stranger donates in a spontaneous, unplanned moment, you can understand the psychology needed to attract and retain any donor, regardless of relationship history.

The Four Motivational Drivers and Their Relevance to Fundraisers

This research examined four motivational constructs rooted in McClelland's Theory of Needs:

1. **Achievement**
   The donor's desire for excellence, measurable impact, and mission effectiveness.
   Fundraising application: donors respond to data, results, measurable outcomes, and organizational competence.

2. **Affiliation**
   The donor's desire to feel connected to a community or shared identity.
   Fundraising application: donors respond to belonging, social connection, and relational engagement.

3. **Philanthropy**
   The internal desire to help others purely for the sake of doing good.
   Fundraising application: donors respond to emotional storytelling, visible need,
   and purpose-driven missions.

4. **Power**
   The desire for influence, recognition, or prestige.
   Fundraising application: donors respond to leadership giving societies, naming
   opportunities, and visible acknowledgment.

The data from this research revealed something groundbreaking for nonprofit
professionals.

Achievement and Philanthropy, not Affiliation or Power, are the strongest predictors of
giving among first-time donors with no prior relationship.

This finding reshapes how nonprofits should approach:

• digital acquisition
• spontaneous giving environments
• first-time donor retention
• visitor experiences
• event-based fundraising
• donor journey design
• capital campaign introductions
• messaging for cold audiences

Understanding these motivations enables you to craft appeals that resonate before a
relationship exists, the key to attracting new donors and converting one-time supporters
into long-term investors.

Why First-Time Donors Matter More Than Ever

The nonprofit sector is facing its most challenging donor landscape in decades. Economic
pressures, decreased household charitable participation, and increased competition have
intensified the need for:

• deeper engagement
• stronger donor journeys
• more effective first-touch experiences

The data is clear:

First-time donors are the least loyal segment and the most expensive to acquire, yet they
represent the largest pool of untapped potential.

When nonprofits understand the motivational triggers that inspired the first gift, they can:

• continue activating those same motivations
• design follow-up strategies that feel personally relevant
• increase repeat giving rates
• strengthen donor identity formation
• build longer donor lifecycles

Motivation is the bridge between initial interest and sustained generosity.

Setting the Stage: The Professional Significance of Donor Motivation

This book provides nonprofit leaders, fundraisers, development directors, and board members with:

• A scientifically grounded framework for understanding why donors give
• A research-backed method for designing donor experiences
• Practical messaging strategies aligned to each motivation
• Guidance for increasing first-time donor conversion and retention
• A roadmap for building long-term donor value

The goal is simple:

To help you inspire more people to give, and to give more meaningfully.

As the research shows:

When nonprofits understand why people give, they dramatically improve how people give.

And when donors feel understood, valued, and aligned with a mission, they do what they have always done throughout history:

They give generously.

They give purposefully.

They give again.

CHAPTER 4: CHAPTER SUMMARIES – WHAT YOU CAN EXPECT

Chapter 1 - Introduction: The Heart of Giving

- Why nonprofits must understand motivation
- The basilica as a unique natural laboratory
- The four motivations (Achievement, Affiliation, Philanthropy, Power)
- Why first-time donors matter
- The moment-based giving model

Setting the Stage: Why Donor Motivation Matters

For the first time in years, donors reduced their monetary contributions as families and businesses tightened budgets. Nonprofits suddenly faced budget cuts, stalled programs, and increased need. An inflationary environment revealed something deeper.

To survive, nonprofits must understand why donors give, especially first-time donors. Many organizations understand how much donors give and when they give. Yet few understand the motivations behind a donor's decision, particularly when that donor has no previous relationship with the organization.

The Four Motivational Drivers

This study examined four motivations:

- **Achievement**: supporting excellence, creating impact
- **Affiliation**: connecting with a community
- **Philanthropy**: doing good for its own sake
- **Power**: desire for influence or recognition

Achievement and philanthropy emerged as the strongest predictors of giving based on this quantitative research.

Chapter 2 – Literature Review: What We Already Know About Donors

- Philanthropic history and economics
- Market failure theory
- Donor fatigue
- Motivation theory (Maslow, Herzberg, McClelland, Bandura)
- Religious motivations for giving
- The psychology of the ask
- The altruism–egoism continuum

Understanding the Human, Social, and Religious Forces Behind Giving

The literature review covered three major bodies of research:

1. Philanthropy Literature

Scholars identified philanthropy as a blend of economics, civic virtue, and altruism. Key insights included:

- People give because nonprofits meet needs markets cannot.
- Charity builds social trust, community identity, and public good.
- Economic conditions heavily influence donor behavior.
- Donor fatigue can reduce giving, especially in tough times.

2. Motivation Literature

Fundraising aligns with multiple psychological theories:

- Maslow's Hierarchy of Needs: giving satisfies higher-level values
- Herzberg's Two-Factor Theory: mission inspires motivators
- McClelland's Theory of Needs: donors want achievement, affiliation, power
- Bandura's Social Learning Theory: giving is influenced by role models
- Altruism vs. Egoism Debate: donors may seek emotional reward

3. Religion in Philanthropy

This research noted:

- Religious individuals give more frequently and more generously.
- The basilica setting activates spiritual motivations.
- Prayer, devotion, and gratitude shape giving behavior.

These insights framed the conceptual foundation of this study.

Chapter 3 – Research Method: How Donor Motivation Was Measured

- Why a quantitative design
- Participant selection (first-time donors only)
- The Strode survey instrument
- Measurement scales and constructs
- Data collection, processing, and statistical analysis

How the Study Was Designed and Why It Matters

This research used:

- A validated quantitative survey instrument (Strode, 2006)
- A target population of 484 donors from outside Florida
- A final sample of 216 respondents (45 percent response rate)

- Independent variables: Achievement, Affiliation, Philanthropy, Power
- Dependent variable: Monetary donation level

The basilica was selected because:

- it has no parishioners,
- no regular giving base,
- and donors have no prior relationship with the organization as first-time donors.

This made the results uniquely applicable to nonprofits seeking first-time donors.

Chapter 4 - Findings: What Donors Actually Told Us

- Demographic snapshot
- Mean scores across all four motivations
- Statistical significance of achievement and philanthropy
- Why affiliation and power did not predict giving
- Surprising findings about tourist donors
- Analysis through motivational theory

What the Data Revealed About Motivations

These findings were clear:

1. Philanthropy (helping others) had the highest motivation score.
Mean = 4.0 (Strong)

2. Achievement (wanting to support excellence) was second.
Mean = 3.7

3. Achievement and Philanthropy were statistically significant predictors of giving.
4. Affiliation and Power mattered emotionally but were not significant predictors of giving levels.

The strongest reasons donors gave:

- They felt their contribution made a difference.
- They believed the basilica was worthy of excellence.
- They wanted to help others or future visitors.
- They were moved spiritually by the basilica environment.

The weakest reasons donors gave:

- Income tax benefits
- Seeking influence
- Insider access

- Social status

Chapter 5 - Discussion: What This Means for Nonprofits

- Applying motivations to fundraising
- Designing donor experiences
- Messaging frameworks for each motivation
- The power of first impressions
- Building sustainable donor journeys
- Recommendations for nonprofit leaders
- Opportunities for future research

What This Means for Fundraising Strategy

This research scientifically and quantitatively proves:

1. Donor motivations can be identified, predicted, and activated.
Nonprofits must design experiences that inspire achievement and philanthropy.

2. Donors without a relationship still give when the mission resonates.

That means nonprofits must prioritize:

- first impressions
- mission clarity
- emotional experience
- communication that connects

3. Spiritual, emotional, and experiential triggers lead to spontaneous giving.

4. Messaging should be motivation driven.

Achievement-Motivated Donors need:

- Impact stories
- Data
- Outcomes
- Excellence

Philanthropy-Motivated Donors need:

- Emotional storytelling
- Visible need
- Clear purpose
- Hope and meaning

5. The future of fundraising lies in understanding why donors give, not just who they are.

CHAPTER 5: DONOR MOTIVATIONS OUTREACH TOOLS

A Technical Framework for Donor Identification and Tailored Fundraising Strategy

TOOL A — Donor Motivation Profiles

Motivation-driven fundraising allows nonprofit professionals to move beyond one-size-fits-all messaging and instead craft precision appeals that align with how donors think, decide, and feel. These four donor profiles translate validated motivational constructs into practical tools fundraisers can use during:

- donor meetings
- cultivation calls
- board interactions
- event engagement
- capital campaign conversations
- annual fund planning
- stewardship touchpoints

By recognizing motivation cues in real time, fundraisers can adjust their language, materials, and call-to-action to dramatically increase conversion, retention, and long-term donor value.

1. Achievement-Motivated Donors - The Investor Mindset

Core Psychological Driver:

Achievement donors are motivated by results, excellence, and measurable impact. They behave like investors rather than patrons. Their satisfaction comes from outcome attainment.

What they care about:

- measurable outcomes
- efficiency and operational competence
- strategic goals and progress dashboards
- quantifiable ROI
- performance compared to peers or benchmarks

Behavioral cues (what fundraisers should watch for):

- They ask "how" questions—how many, how fast, how efficiently
- They want comparisons: year over year, program vs. program, cost per impact
- They reference performance, quality, or organizational effectiveness
- They show interest in strategic plans, key performance indicators (KPIs), or logic models

How to engage them (best messaging frames):

• "Your gift will directly achieve…"
• "Here is the measurable progress your investment unlocks."
• "Let me show you our data trends, benchmarks, and milestones."
• "We track outcomes rigorously, and here is the evidence."

Best stewardship strategies:

• quarterly or semi-annual impact dashboards
• performance reviews with program staff
• site visits focused on operational excellence
• access to strategic planning updates
• charts, metrics, and before-after data visualizations

Real-World Fundraising Application:

Achievement donors thrive in capital campaigns, program scaling initiatives, innovation funds, measurable intervention programs, and high-ROI projects. Treat them like strategic partners, not passive supporters.

2. Affiliation-Motivated Donors - The Community-Builders

Core Psychological Driver:

Affiliation donors give because they want to belong. Their motivation is rooted in connection, identity, and relationship experience, not data or outcomes.

What they care about:

• social connection
• community identity
• shared experiences
• volunteer culture
• relationships with staff, supporters, and participants

Behavioral cues:

• They emphasize "we," "our," or "together."
• They gravitate toward events, gatherings, and community activities.
• They ask questions about people, not metrics.
• They inquire about opportunities to engage, volunteer, or join groups.

How to engage them:

• "We would love for you to be part of this community."
• "You will be joining a network of passionate supporters."
• "Let me introduce you to others who share your values."
• "Your presence strengthens our mission family."

Best stewardship strategies:

• personal thank-you calls from staff or volunteers
• invitations to mission circles, ambassador groups, or affinity clubs
• intimate behind-the-scenes gatherings
• volunteer roles where they can connect with others

Real-World Fundraising Application:

Affiliation donors excel in annual fund societies, peer-to-peer fundraising, community events, volunteer-driven campaigns, and donor networks. Strengthen their sense of belonging, and their giving will deepen.

3. Philanthropy-Motivated Donors - The Purpose-Driven Givers

Core Psychological Driver:

Philanthropy donors give to express values, compassion, and moral purpose. Their motivation is rooted in meaning, empathy, and the desire to help others.

What they care about:

• improving lives
• mission alignment
• values, faith, and purpose
• emotional connection to the cause
• visible impact on people, not systems

Behavioral cues:

• They talk about values: kindness, hope, justice, compassion.
• They respond emotionally to stories, testimonies, and visuals.
• They ask "who" questions more than "how many."
• They reference personal experiences, family influences, or faith.

How to engage them:

• "Your generosity gives hope to…"
• "Let me share the story of someone whose life changed."

• "Your compassion creates real transformation."
• "You are restoring dignity, healing, or opportunity."

Best stewardship strategies:

• handwritten notes
• gratitude videos
• personal stories of those helped
• mission-first updates and inspirational impact moments

Real-World Fundraising Application:

These donors respond powerfully to annual appeals, holiday campaigns, legacy giving, humanitarian programs, compassion-driven missions, emergency relief, and faith-based giving environments.

4. Power-Motivated Donors - The Leaders and Influencers

Core Psychological Driver:

Power-motivated donors seek influence, leadership, and recognition. They want to shape outcomes, not just fund them. Their motivation is rooted in agency, status affirmation, and strategic involvement.

What they care about:

• visibility
• influence and access
• decision-making opportunity
• leadership roles
• high-level recognition

Behavioral cues:

• They ask how they can help guide, shape, or advise.
• They want to meet executives, board chairs, or program directors.
• They ask questions about governance, strategy, or leadership direction.
• They show interest in naming opportunities, sponsorship levels, or VIP access.

How to engage them:

• "Your leadership could significantly advance this effort."
• "We would value your strategic insight on this initiative."
• "Let's explore a leadership role or naming opportunity."
• "You would be part of a select group shaping the future."

Best stewardship strategies:

• executive-level communication
• early access to announcements
• special recognitions and acknowledgments
• invitations to join committees, task forces, or boards

Real-World Fundraising Application:

Power donors are ideal for major gifts, capital campaigns, innovation councils, leadership gifts, strategic initiatives, sponsorship packages, and board recruitment pipelines.

How Fundraisers Should Use These Profiles

This tool becomes dramatically more powerful when incorporated into:

1. **Donor Meeting Prep**
Identify likely motivation based on research, giving history, or pre-meeting notes.

2. **Real-Time Conversation Adjustment**
Shift your language and framing based on cues you observe.

3. **Customized Stewardship Plans**
Build individualized stewardship sequences aligned to the donor's core motivation.

4. **Campaign Messaging Architecture**
Segment communication by motivation type.

For example:

• Achievement = data-heavy annual report

• Philanthropy = mission story in holiday appeal

• Affiliation = event invitation

• Power = leadership briefing

5. **Digital Donor Journeys**

Motivation-based segmentation dramatically increases email conversion and acquisition ROI.

6. **Board Member Training**

Equip board members with these profiles so they can tailor their peer-to-peer asks.

TOOL B — Motivation-Based Communication Scripts

These scripts are not generic templates. They are strategic communication frameworks grounded in motivational theory, behavioral economics, and donor psychology. Each script is engineered to:

- increase donor conversion
- deepen emotional resonance
- align messaging with internal motivation
- accelerate donor movement through the giving cycle
- improve long-term retention

Use them in email appeals, discovery calls, donor visits, board fundraising, capital campaigns, or stewardship communications.

Achievement Donor Script for the "The Impact Investor"

Technical Insight:

Achievement donors respond to cognitive triggers: measurable impact, operational excellence, and clear ROI. They activate the brain's "reward for outcome" pathways.

Ask Script (Email / Phone / Meeting):

"Your support will directly help us achieve ___ by ___. With your investment, we can accelerate progress, reach this critical milestone, and deliver measurable outcomes. Here are the quantifiable results your generosity makes possible…"

What this script does:

- uses causal language ("your support will directly…")
- emphasizes milestones and results
- positions donor as a strategic partner

Stewardship Follow-Up:

"I wanted to personally share the measurable results you helped create. Because of your gift, we accomplished ___. Your investment is producing real, provable impact."

Best practice:

Send dashboards, metrics, before-and-after charts, or program scorecards.

Affiliation Donor Script for "The Community Builder"

Technical Insight:

Affiliation donors are motivated by connection, belonging, and shared identity. Social neuroscience shows these donors respond to group inclusion cues.

Ask Script:

"You belong here. This mission is stronger because of caring people like you. We would be honored to welcome you into this community of supporters who make a difference together."

What this script does:

• invokes identity ("you belong here")
• emphasizes community over transaction
• uses warm, relational language

Stewardship Follow-Up:

"Thank you again for being part of our mission family. Here's what your community of supporters helped achieve this month…"

Best practice:

Tie their gift to group success, not individual recognition.

Philanthropy Donor Script for "The Purpose-Driven Giver"

Technical Insight:

Philanthropy donors are motivated by compassion, moral purpose, and values. Emotional storytelling is their strongest motivator.

Ask Script:

"Your generosity will bring hope to ___ and change lives immediately. Your kindness has the power to create real transformation today."

What this script does:

• appeals to empathy and moral identity
• uses hope-based language
• focuses on human impact rather than systems

Stewardship Follow-Up:

"I wanted to share the difference your kindness made for ___. Your compassion is changing lives."

Best practice:

Use human-centered stories, photographs, and gratitude videos.

Power Donor Script for "The Strategic Leader"

Technical Insight:

Power donors value influence, recognition, and strategic involvement. They respond to language emphasizing leadership, agency, and partnership.

Ask Script:

"We are seeking leaders who can help shape the future of this project. Your involvement at the strategic level would make an extraordinary impact."

What this script does:

- frames the donor as a leader
- signals exclusivity and influence
- appeals to desire for agency and visibility

Stewardship Follow-Up:

"Your leadership is deeply valued. We would appreciate your insight in our next strategic discussion about ___."

Best practice:

Invite them to advisory councils, briefings, or VIP meetings.

TOOL C — Donor Survey Instrument

A Motivation Identification Tool Built for Nonprofits

This survey is designed for immediate deployment through:

• Google Forms
• SurveyMonkey
• QR codes at events
• email cultivation sequences
• donor onboarding packets
• annual stewardship surveys

It provides quantitative motivational data you can track year over year.

Quick Donor Motivation Survey

(1 = Strongly Disagree, 5 = Strongly Agree)

Achievement Motivation
1. My donation helps accomplish something important.
2. I give when I believe the organization performs at a high level.
3. I want my gift to contribute to measurable results.

Affiliation Motivation
4. I give because I feel connected to this organization.
5. Being part of this mission matters to me.
6. I want to belong to a community of supporters.

Philanthropy Motivation
7. I give because helping others is important to me.
8. I believe giving is the right thing to do.
9. I am motivated by compassion.

Power Motivation
10. I like having influence in the organizations I support.
11. I appreciate recognition for my giving.
12. I enjoy being involved in leadership roles.

Open-Ended Questions

• What inspired your recent gift?
• How do you prefer to be thanked or recognized?
• What could we do to strengthen our relationship with you?

How to Use This Instrument

1. Motivation Scoring

• Identify the donor's highest-scoring category.
• Secondary motivations can refine messaging, especially for major donors.

2. Communication Adjustment

• Achievement → send data-driven appeals
• Affiliation → invite to events
• Philanthropy → tell impact stories
• Power → offer leadership involvement

3. Annual Trend Tracking

Analyze shifts in motivations over time to adjust:

• campaign messaging
• donor journey design
• board member scripts
• stewardship calendars

4. Major Gift Qualification

Motivation scores are strong predictors of:

• donor capacity
• donor intent
• long-term loyalty
• willingness to upgrade

TOOL D — The Annual Fundraising Blueprint

A 12-Month Implementation Framework

This is a field-tested, motivation-driven annual fundraising plan that integrates your donor data with donor psychology and strategic communication.

Step 1 — Set Motivation-Based Goals

Use Tool A (Motivation Profiles) to segment your donor base into:

- Achievement
- Affiliation
- Philanthropy
- Power

For each segment, set:

- revenue goals
- retention targets
- engagement objectives
- stewardship frequency

Step 2 — Build a 12-Month Motivation Messaging Calendar

Assign one motivational theme per month to systematically engage every donor type.

Monthly Themes:

> **Jan:** Impact Metrics (Achievement)
> **Feb:** Community Love Stories (Affiliation)
> **Mar:** Compassion Campaign (Philanthropy)
> **Apr:** Leadership Briefings (Power)
> **May:** Volunteer Appreciation (Affiliation)
> **Jun:** Summer Impact Push (Achievement)
> **Jul:** Mission Storytelling (Philanthropy)
> **Aug:** Advisory Council Recruitment (Power)
> **Sept:** Back-to-School Impact (Achievement)
> **Oct:** Fall Gatherings and Donor Mixers (Affiliation)
> **Nov:** Giving Season Inspiration (Philanthropy)
> **Dec:** Year-End Leadership Circle (Power)

Professional Benefit:

This ensures balanced cultivation rather than overreliance on a single donor type.

Step 3 — Implement Stewardship Systems

Every donor receives:

• a timely, personalized thank-you
• quarterly impact updates
• at least one personal touch per year
• a motivation-specific message

Example:

A Philanthropy donor receives a heartfelt story.

An Achievement donor receives a performance update.

Step 4 — Empower Your Board

Provide board members with:

• motivation-based talking points
• scripts from Tool B
• donor lists aligned with each board member's strengths
• monthly call assignments
• peer-to-peer training

Board members become much more effective fundraisers when they communicate in their natural motivational language.

Step 5 — Evaluate Quarterly

Monitor:

• retention by segment
• average gift growth
• donor upgrade patterns
• motivation shifts
• response rates to messaging
• monthly cultivation engagement

This data drives continuous improvement and predictable revenue growth.

CHAPTER 6: QUALITATIVE RESEARCH ABSTRACT

Nonprofit leaders and development staff must understand what motivates donors to contribute a monetary donation. This quantitative study statistically analyzed the motivations of achievement, affiliation, philanthropy, and power (independent variables) of donors who provided a monetary donation (dependent variable) to a nonprofit without having a previous relationship. Quantitative data represented the personal motivations of individual donors (tourists) providing a monetary donation to a nonprofit Roman Catholic basilica in Florida. To ensure validity the sample did not have a previous relationship with the nonprofit, only first-time donors living outside Florida who provided a monetary donation to the basilica were selected to participate in the survey. A survey of the target population of 484 donors living outside of the basilica's home state of Florida resulted in a sample of 216 participants representing 45% of the target population. The motivations of achievement, affiliation, philanthropy, and power were analyzed with an analysis of variance and a single regression analysis. An analysis of variance showed there was a significant effect of achievement and philanthropy on the donor's monetary donation at the p<.05 level for the three conditions F (3, 212) = 4.07, p = .003 and F (3, 212) = 2.97, p = .020 respectively. A descriptive statistical analysis indicated the motivations of philanthropy (M=4.0, SD=.62) and achievement (M=3.7, SD=.83) resulted in the highest mean scores of the four independent variables. The single regression significantly predicted achievement scores β = -.23, t(3.38) = .00, p < .05 and philanthropy scores β = -.16, t(2.39) = .02, p < .05. The data from this analysis can assist nonprofit organizations structure development campaigns to appeal to specific donor motivations. Future research can create further understanding of specific donor motivations to provide monetary donations to nonprofits in other circumstances than donors who did not have a previous relationship.

CHAPTER 7: INTRODUCTION

Decreased monetary donations to nonprofit organizations have forced nonprofits to reevaluate development strategies to react to the financial constraints of donors caused by the economic recession (Arcieri, 2009). Declining home sales, the reluctance of employers to hire new staff, and volatile world stock markets resulted in an inflationary United States economy (Semuels, 2010). In the United States throughout 2008, the total estimated nonprofit monetary donations were $307.65 billion, down 2% from a record $314.07 billion in 2007 after 20 consecutive years of continual growth (Arcieri, 2009). Nonprofit entities almost exclusively rely on the philanthropic support of individual donors as decreased monetary donations have occurred (Henke & Fontenot, 2009). Philanthropic support, or altruistic helping behavior, includes providing of monetary donations from corporations, trusts, foundations, and individual donors. Consistent monetary donations to a nonprofit are critical for the nonprofit organization to achieve financial sustainability. Understanding the motivation of an individual donor to contribute a monetary donation is critical to successful nonprofit fundraising endeavors. The motivations of individual donors help define philanthropy, or a charitable assistance behavior, through the act of providing a monetary donation to a nonprofit organization.

The basis of this research was a quantitative analysis on the motivations of donors providing a monetary donation to a nonprofit without a previous relationship. The research included theoretical frameworks derived from literature associated with sales and marketing as well as multiple motivational theories. Individual donors in the United States account for over 75% of all nonprofit donations provided to nonprofits each year (Henke & Fontenot, 2009). Because individual donors contribute for themselves, or on behalf of a family, trust, or business, understanding individual donor motivations is essential to future nonprofit development success and donor outreach. The nonprofit organizations are behaving like for-profit businesses because of the influence and implementation of traditional sales and marketing practices treating the donor as a customer.

Because of the recent economic inflation and financial constraints in the United States, the philanthropic community is operating like traditional for-profit businesses (Arcieri, 2009). Nonprofit organizations are viewing their donors as customers. Nonprofit organizations create stronger customer relationships by developing strategic marketing initiatives focused on the donor as a customer and business partner. The results obtained from the valid and reliable quantitative survey instrument from this study can help predict motivations of specific individual donors that can create fundraising strategies and development programs for the nonprofit. The creation of fundraising campaigns for nonprofits based on specific motivations of donors can increase monetary donations generated by the nonprofit (Strode, 2006).

This chapter outlines the motivation of donors providing a philanthropic monetary donation, the motivational role of religion on philanthropic monetary donations, and psychological and behavioral motivational theories leading to the altruistic behaviors of providing monetary donations to a nonprofit. Research in the philanthropy and motivation subject areas helped create the theoretical framework applied within this study to describe motivations of a donor to provide a monetary donation when the donor did not have a previous relationship with the nonprofit. This chapter includes a summary on the background of philanthropic motivational research providing the foundation to answer each of the respective research questions, test each of the null and alternative hypotheses, in addition to highlighting the significance of this quantitative study.

Background

The analysis of why individual donors choose to provide a monetary donation to a nonprofit has served as a basis of philanthropy research in the disciplines of economics, psychology, social psychology, sociology, and anthropology (Sargeant & Woodliffe, 2007). Sargeant and Woodliffe (2007) stated that traditional philanthropy and fundraising disciplines are increasingly incorporating psychology and motivational analysis into traditional management and marketing research. Management, marketing, and development operations of a nonprofit organization incorporate data analysis from research to help predict future monetary donations from donors. A nonprofit organization's development staff can apply research to create specific marketing initiatives and donor development campaigns that encapsulate specific donor motives (Arcieri, 2009). Knowledge of specific donor motivations could provide the nonprofit organization a predictable monetary donation return on the nonprofits' fundraising campaign investments (Strode, 2006).

Leaders at nonprofit organizations require the capacity, infrastructure, and brand recognition to contend for grants, corporate or government partnerships, sponsorships, and major gifts from individuals (Shaw & Shaw, 2008). Judgments made on the performance of nonprofit leaders focus exclusively on abilities to grow endowments, increase donation rates, secure monetary funds, and manage capital campaigns with accountability measures much for-profit businesses (Shaw & Shaw, 2008). The donor motivation analysis received from a valid and reliable survey is an advantage to the staff of a nonprofit to predict motivations based upon donor demographics such as gender, age, income level, and the monetary donation level. In recessionary economic times, Scott (2010) stated high morale of employees at a nonprofit organization is a benefit to organizational productivity, which directly benefits the donors. Nonprofits need to possess accurate donor profiles and valid information, which permits increased efficiency in donor development efforts and a positive attitude in nonprofit work environment.

Frequently, individuals receive unsolicited materials from nonprofit organizations via the United States Postal Service, telephone, or electronic mail as a part of soliciting potential donors without a previous relationship with the nonprofit. Many national nonprofits send unsolicited collateral fundraising materials in the mail such as the American Red Cross, the American Lung Association, and the Humane Society of the United States. Many nonprofit organizations could benefit from information on the motives of donors to provide a monetary donation when the prospective donor did not have a previous relationship with the nonprofit (Strode, 2006).

Donors are providing fewer monetary donations in both total dollar amount and frequency within a fragile United States recessionary economy (Arcieri, 2009). Nonprofits are overhauling organizational fundraising strategies to attract more donors to increase monetary donation amounts and frequencies (Arcieri, 2009). For the first time in more than two decades, American philanthropic monetary donations were down in 2008 (Arcieri, 2009). Appealing directly to specific donor motivations in a recessionary economic environment allows the nonprofit to target and appeal to specific donor motivations in future marketing, development, and fundraising campaigns with increased efficiency.

Arcieri (2009) stated that nonprofits are making donor contacts more personal, appealing directly to the donor as a unique individual. Arcieri contended that creating a nonprofit organizational relationship with donors involved conducting more stewardship campaigns. Nonprofit organizations are maintaining connections with prospective and current donors in addition to spending more time demonstrating appreciation for current donors. According to

Durando (2010), 62% of American participants surveyed reported they planned to match their

individual donation levels from 2009. The Durando survey results indicated that 10% of

participants planned to donate more monetarily than their total amounts in 2009 to nonprofits,

whereas 23% responded they intended to give less. The Durando research supported the Arcieri

(2009) findings of a decline in monetary donations to nonprofit organizations from donors.

Problem Statement

In a recessionary United States economy, current donors are decreasing monetary

donations to nonprofit organizations (Arcieri, 2009). As a result, nonprofit organizations seek to

attract new donors to replace the decreasing monetary donations by current nonprofit donors

(Arcieri, 2009). Nonprofits must rethink development strategies to attract new donors as well as

retain current donors (Durando, 2010). Understanding a donor's motivation to provide a

monetary donation to a nonprofit is critical for the organization to achieve the necessary

philanthropic monetary donations. Analysis on the motivations of donors who provide a

monetary donation to a nonprofit without a previous relationship would assist nonprofits in their

attempts to attract new donors. This study statistically analyzed the motivations of achievement,

affiliation, philanthropy, and power of donors who provided a monetary donation to a nonprofit

without having a previous relationship. Research conducted to help understand donor

motivations to provide a monetary donation to a nonprofit organization facilitated the

exploration, comparison, and understanding of donor motivations in this study (Burton, 2010;

Gaulke, 2010; Lackie, 2010; Mahoney, Gladden, & Funk, 2003; Staurowsky, Parkhouse, &

Sachs, 1996; Strode, 2006; Verner, Hecht, & Fansler, 1998).

Research of donor motivations does not provide a singular and reliable motivational theoretical basis. Comprehending a variety of motivational theories is necessary to describe relationships between different donor motivations to provide a monetary donation to a nonprofit where the donor does not have a previous relationship with a nonprofit. Motivational theory based on the Mahoney et al. (2003) and Strode (2006) research is applicable to describe the donor's motivation to provide a monetary donation to a nonprofit. This study will highlight numerous studies on philanthropic research theories traditionally associated with sales and marketing, and integrated with human motivation and religion philanthropic theories, provided explanations for a donor to provide a monetary donation to a nonprofit.

Purpose

The purpose of this quantitative study was to describe the relationships between the achievement, affiliation, philanthropy, and power motivations of donors to provide a monetary donation to a nonprofit without having a previous relationship. Comparisons were made of personal motivations of the target population of donors who provided a monetary donation to a nonprofit Roman Catholic basilica without a previous relationship based on the donor's monetary donation level. The four motives of achievement, affiliation, philanthropy, and power (independent variables) relative to the monetary donation level (dependent variable) were analyzed. This study incorporated, with permission, Strode's (2006) survey instrument that used multiple motivational theoretical frameworks to test donor motivations providing monetary donations to a nonprofit.

The Strode (2006) survey was selected for this study because the instrument was validated to provide data from participant's responses to statistically test data from this study with an analysis of variance (ANOVA) and a single regression analysis. Strode's (2006) validated and reliable survey instrument was designed by Strode to minimize respondent error that established the data collected from the survey was accurate and truthful based on quantitative research theory. Strode's (2006) study focused on the creation of a psychometrically sound survey instrument based on motivational theory that can be used to create donor motivation profiles for nonprofit organizations. Strode's (2006) psychometrically valid quantitative survey instrument was sent to the target population of 484 donors who reside outside of Florida and provided a monetary donation to a nonprofit basilica resulting in a sample of 216 participants. The nonprofit basilica in the study serves tourists and guests in a city in Florida. The target population only included donors who did not have a previous relationship with the basilica.

Theoretical Framework

Understanding theoretical perspectives of quantitative research methods relative to the analysis of donor motivations providing a monetary donation to a nonprofit was critical to this research. The participants in the sample from this study provided statistical evidence by self-reporting information with the survey instrument, developed and used with permission by Strode (2006). The quantitative data accumulated from the analysis of motivations of basilica donors fits with other quantitative research (Burton, 2010; Gaulke, 2010; Lackie, 2010, Maynard, 2008; Yuruk, 2008; Cugliari, 2005; Schortgen, 2006; Strode, 2006). The data from this study tested the hypotheses, thus answering the respective research questions based on multiple motivational theories with motivations of achievement, affiliation, philanthropy, and power.

Observations of relationships between donor motivations providing a monetary donation to a nonprofit in this quantitative research tested hypotheses though the use of measurements and testing theories (Creswell, 2009). Applications of quantitative research frameworks used in research of the motivations of donors providing monetary donations to nonprofits within the business development field guided this study (Burton, 2010; Cugliari, 2005; Gaulke, 2010; Lackie, 2010, Maynard, 2008; Schortgen, 2006; Strode, 2006; Yuruk, 2008). The comparative quantitative research used quantitative data on predetermined, valid, and reliable survey instrument developed by Strode (2006) that tested statistical data self-reported by participants in the sample (Creswell, 2009). Quantitative research design required this study to test data based on philanthropic research theories traditionally associated with sales and marketing, and multiple motivational and religion philanthropic theories. These theoretical frameworks provided research examples of the motivations of donors to provide a monetary donation to a specific nonprofit. The applied research approach was the most beneficial for this comparative quantitative study to analyze the motives of participant donors who provided a monetary donation to the basilica without a previous relationship.

Maynard (2008) explained that fundraising has focused on the basic tenant of receiving an immediate monetary donation from the donor. This immediate transactional fundraising definition is similar with Kelly (1991), who stated that fundraising is a process of soliciting and accepting monetary gifts from individuals, corporations, and foundations by nonprofit organizations. Conversely, true philanthropy, unlike fundraising, must focus on developing the future relationship with the individual donor, not simply obtaining the immediate monetary donation (Maynard, 2008). The words charity and philanthropy are synonymous in literature as each involves individuals offering altruistic helping behaviors, usually in the form of providing a monetary donation to a nonprofit (Cugliari, 2005).

Feingold (1987) defined philanthropy as charity by offering support to those in need, supporting the synonymous nature of the definition and meaning of charity and philanthropy.

Maynard (2008) stated that nonprofits, incorporating a futuristic philanthropic relationship approach, find that monetary donations would occur after securing the personal commitment from the individual donor. Establishing a true philanthropic relationship is critical, as the individual donor must be personally motivated to commit to the mission and vision of the nonprofit into the future (Maynard, 2008).

Sargeant and Woodliffe (2007) and Bendapudi, Singh, and Bendapudi (1995) illustrated the for-profit business focus of nonprofits classified by philanthropic research involving the three traditional business-related disciplines of economics, marketing, and social psychology. In the relationship between the individual donor and the beneficiary of a monetary donation or gift, Bendapudi et al. affirmed that economists and researchers have been predisposed to observe the monetary donation in philanthropic research. However, evaluating the motivation of donors through their altruistic helping behavior of providing a monetary donation is important in developing a customer relationship (Bendapudi et al., 1995).

The previous research examples focus on the dynamics of fundraising efforts with Maynard's (2008) explanations on immediate transactional fundraising and future oriented relationships of philanthropy. Because of current recessionary economic conditions and financial constraints for individuals and businesses (Arcieri, 2009), philanthropic organizations are operating like for-profit businesses as customer relationship and consumer marketing initiatives are incorporated by nonprofit organizations (Woodliffe, 2007). The use of customer relationship frameworks in sales and marketing endeavors extends to viewing individual donors as customers by focusing on the donor relationships with the nonprofit (Lacey, 2007). The customer relationship theory provides economic, social, and resource flexibility to individual donors of a nonprofit while providing the nonprofit an explanation of the motivations behind a donor providing a monetary donation (Lacey, 2007).

Waters (2007) stated individual donors account for 80% of revenue to nonprofits from research that focused on a customer driven donor theory. Because the majority of nonprofits' budget comes from individuals, it is critical for nonprofit organizations to create strong future oriented relationships with their donors to provide monetary donations (Waters, 2007). Waters revealed that positive public relations customer drivers provide a theoretical framework to evaluate the donor motivations to provide a monetary donation as well as the relationship between the nonprofit and donor. Waters' research supported the Lacey (2007) study with the need for nonprofits to establish strong customer relationship frameworks with theoretical frameworks associated with sales and marketing by for-profit organizations.

Research Questions

In a setting where donors did not have a previous relationship with a nonprofit, this research incorporated a survey instrument that implemented a quantitative Likert-type scale developed by Strode (2006) to collect data from a target population of 484 donors who provided a monetary donation to a basilica in Florida. A test of the sample of 216 participant donors who provided a monetary donation to the basilica revealed if statistical differences exist among the motivations based on McClelland's (1961) theory of needs, in addition to the altruistic helping motive of philanthropy based on Strode's (2006) research. A statistical test on the raw data collected from participants self-reporting information through the survey instrument analyzed the donor motivations (independent variables) of achievement, affiliation, and power on the monetary donation level (dependent variable). The dependent variable is the categorized donor monetary donation level amount using the participant's self-reported information.

Q1. Is there a statistical difference of the variance among the four motives of achievement, affiliation, philanthropy, and power relative to the level of the monetary donation?

Q2. Is there a statistical correlation between the motivation of achievement on the monetary donation level of a donor who did not have a previous relationship with the nonprofit?

Q3. Is there a statistical correlation between the motivation of affiliation on the monetary donation level of a donor who did not have a previous relationship with the nonprofit?

Q4. Is there a statistical correlation between the motivation of philanthropy on the monetary donation level of a donor who did not have a previous relationship with the nonprofit?

Q5. Is there a statistical correlation between the motivation of power on the monetary donation level of a donor who did not have a previous relationship with the nonprofit?

Hypotheses

$H1_0$. There is no statistical difference of the variance among the four motivations of achievement, affiliation, philanthropy, and power relative to the level of the monetary donation.

$H1_a$. There is a statistical difference of the variance among the four motivations of achievement, affiliation, philanthropy, and power relative to the level of the monetary donation.

$H2_0$. There is no statistical correlation between the motivation of achievement relative to the level of the monetary donation.

H2$_a$. There is a statistical correlation between the motivation of achievement relative to the level of the monetary donation.

H3$_0$. There is no statistical correlation between the motivation of affiliation relative to the level of the monetary donation.

H3$_a$. There is a statistical correlation between the motivation of affiliation relative to the level of the monetary donation.

H4$_0$. There is no statistical correlation between the motivation of philanthropy relative to the level of the monetary donation.

H4$_a$. There is a statistical correlation between the motivation of philanthropy relative to the level of the monetary donation.

H5$_0$. There is no statistical correlation between the motivation of power relative to the level of the monetary donation.

H5$_a$. There is a statistical correlation between the motivation of power relative to the level of the monetary donation.

The objective of the respective research questions in this study offers descriptions of the relationships between the donor motivations of achievement, affiliation, philanthropy, and power with donors who did not have a previous relationship with the nonprofit based on the monetary donation level. This study included quantitative data to describe results from the analysis of the different motivations of the sample donors. The four motivations achievement, affiliation, philanthropy, and power (independent variables) based on the donors' monetary donation level (dependent variable) to a nonprofit basilica, tested theories traditionally associated with sales and marketing along with multiple motivational theories to describe why an individual is compelled to provide a monetary donation to a specific nonprofit without a previous relationship.

The motivations of achievement, affiliation, and power based on McClelland's (1961) theory of needs, along with the altruistic helping motive of philanthropy implemented by Strode (2006), comprised the independent variables incorporated in the survey instrument. The categorized monetary donation levels self-reported by the participants represent the dependent variables in this study. Operational definitions of the dependent (level of monetary donation) and independent variables (motivations of achievement, affiliation, philanthropy, and power) appear later in this chapter after the significance of the research. The survey instrument incorporated a Likert-type scale to collect interval data using a sample of 216 participants from the target population of 484 donors.

This study used Strode's (2006) survey instrument, with permission, to collect data to measure motivations of donors providing a monetary donation to a nonprofit without a previous relationship. Strode's survey instrument incorporated McClelland's theory of needs as the theoretical framework, implementing McClelland's needs of achievement, affiliation, and power along with the altruistic helping motive of philanthropy (Strode, 2006). Klebanow and Lowenkopf (1991) explored how monetary donations attributed to an individual donor related to the donor's motivation of power. Individual donors with large financial resources frequently use their monetary resources as a means to achieve power as well as creating a sense of personal achievement (Strode, 2006).

Furnham and Argyle (1998) stated a positive relationship between individual wealth and providing monetary donations to nonprofits. However, Furnham and Argyle (1998) observed that Americans at the top and bottom of personal income levels provide monetary donations at the same frequency (Strode, 2006). Donors providing monetary donations to nonprofits at the highest and lowest monetary donation levels are also similar in frequency (Strode, 2006).

However, the motives associated with donors providing a monetary donation may be different (Strode, 2006). This study hypothesizes a difference in motives of achievement, affiliation, philanthropy, and power between the five monetary donation levels outlined in the interval Likert-type scales in the survey instrument using an analysis of variance (ANOVA) and a single regression analysis.

Nature of the Study

Within this comparative quantitative study, an analysis of variance (ANOVA) tested the data of independent variables (achievement, affiliation, philanthropy, and power) with the dependent variable (the level of donation). An ANOVA determined statistical significance between the differences in means occurring between two or more groups (Zikmund, Babin, Carr, & Griffin, 2009). This comparative quantitative study was analyzed using a psychometrically valid quantitative cross-sectional survey instrument developed by Strode (2006) based on McClelland's (1961) theory of needs. The quantitative data gathered from the survey instrument incorporating a Likert-type scale collected interval data to test the means of the independent variables with the dependent variable using an ANOVA to test the hypotheses in the study.

To determine if the respective donor motives of achievement, affiliation, philanthropy, and power are significant to the monetary donation level, this study incorporated a single regression analysis. Addition to the single regression analysis, this study utilized descriptive statistics and an ANOVA providing quantitative evidence to help describe the statistical differences between the groups of donors representing the four motivations (the independent variables of achievement, affiliation, philanthropy, and power) based on the donors' level of a monetary donation to a nonprofit basilica in Florida. Participants who had no previous relationship with the nonprofit self-reported their respective individual donor's level of donation (dependent variable) to the basilica through the survey instrument.

The ANOVA used in this study determined if statistically significant differences in means occurred between two or more groups using quantitative research analysis to describe the relationships between the donor motivations in providing a monetary donation to a nonprofit without a previous relationship with the donor (Zikmund et al., 2009). A single regression analysis is a statistical test that outlines the typical value of the dependent variable when any one of the independent variables is varied (Lind et al., 2011). Research studies include a single regression analysis to find the significance of the independent variables with the dependent variable while exploring the relationships (Zikmund et al., 2009).

A single regression analysis used in this study is a statistical test that identifies the statistical correlation between a dependent variable and an independent variable (Lind et al., 2011). An X and Y-axis graph with a straight-line regression equation represent a quantitative test (Lind et al., 2011). The statistical correlations between the variables incorporated data used to develop an estimated regression equation (Lind et al., 2011). The purpose of single regression analysis applied in this study evaluated the effects of one independent variable on a single dependent variable. Lind et al. (2011) stated that even though a correlation exists between two variables, a statistical correlation is not causation. Zikmund et al. (2009) stated a regression study formulates a hypothesis about the relationship between the variables. Using a single regression analysis, this study analyzed statistical correlations between the respective motivations of achievement, affiliation, philanthropy, and power (independent variable) with the monetary donation level (dependent variable).

Significance of the Research

Nonprofits leaders must rethink philanthropic fundraising development strategies to attract and retain donors in a recessionary economic environment in the United States (Arcieri, 2009). Understanding a donor's psychological motivation to provide a nonprofit with monetary donations is critical for the nonprofit's development personnel to maintain sufficient funding for the organization's nonprofit mission. Strode (2006) developed an instrument that measured donor's motivations based on McClelland's (1961) theory of needs, in addition to the motive of philanthropy or an altruistic helping behavior (Strode, 2006). This study implemented the Strode (2006) survey instrument to expand on the Strode research adding new knowledge to compare motivations of donor who provided a monetary donation without a previous relationship with the nonprofit organization.

The contribution of new knowledge from this comparative quantitative research is the analysis of personal donor motivations of achievement, affiliation, philanthropy, and power to help describe motivations of individual donors providing a monetary donation to a nonprofit Roman Catholic Basilica in Florida without a previous relationship. Academic researchers have examined data on individual motivations to provide a monetary donation to various nonprofits organizations including stand-alone churches and single religious congregations. Numerous philanthropic and donor development studies have offered that donor motivations are related providing a monetary donation to a nonprofit.

The studies outlined in research literature in the next chapter focused on donor motivations and not the relationship with the monetary donation level. Two studies (Mahony et al., 2003; Strode, 2006) empirically tested the relationship of the motivations of donors providing a monetary donation to a nonprofit as implemented by this study. However, this quantitative comparative study is significant as these findings added new knowledge to the business development field by analyzing the donor motivations of donors providing a monetary donation to a nonprofit organization, which the donors did not have a previous relationship with the nonprofit organization.

The results from this study explain the motivations of donors using theoretical frameworks derived from literature identified with sales and marketing along with multiple motivational theories. Within academic research, studies outlined information on the motivations of why individuals provide monetary donations to various nonprofits as evident with the research previously highlighted in this study (Burton, 2010; Gaulke, 2010; Lackie, 2010; Mahoney, Gladden, & Funk, 2003; Staurowsky, Parkhouse, & Sachs, 1996; Strode, 2006; Verner, Hecht, & Fansler, 1998). However, this research is significant because this study added new knowledge to business development research by examining the specific motives of donors providing a monetary donation to a nonprofit without a previous relationship not addressed in previous research.

There is additional significance with the nonprofit used in this study, as the nonprofit Roman Catholic Basilica, serving tourists in the state of Florida, does not have any parishioners, nor does the basilica receive any financial support from the local Catholic diocese, according to the basilica's rector Father E. J. McCarthy (personal communication, July 26, 2009). The philanthropic support of the basilica relies almost exclusively on the financial generosity of the individual guests and visitors who come during family vacations or business conventions (Father E. J. McCarthy, personal communication, March 7, 2009). The basilica is the only Catholic house of worship in the world created specifically for tourists in the over 2000-year history of the Roman Catholic Church (Father E. J. McCarthy, personal communication, March 7, 2009).

Originally built as a national shrine, Pope Benedict XVI officially elevated the shrine to a basilica in July 2009 (Father E. J. McCarthy, personal communication, July 26, 2009). Sixty-nine basilicas are located in the United States, of which three basilicas are in the state of Florida, and two of the three Florida-based basilicas, including the one used in this study, are within the same local Catholic dioceses (E. J. McCarthy, personal communication, July 26, 2009).

Donors not having a previous relationship yet providing a monetary donation to the unique nonprofit Roman Catholic basilica in Florida ensure new research significance. The basis for this research significance was visitors who choose to provide a monetary donation to the basilica while on vacation or business trips not having a previous relationship with the nonprofit. Some of the visitors to the basilica did not understand the basilica existed before arriving at their vacation or convention destination in Florida (Father E.J. McCarthy, personal communication, March 7, 2009). The conditions at the basilica of not having any parishioners while serving tourists and visitors in Florida provide a compelling setting in conducting new business research seeking comparative differences among the four motives of achievement, affiliation, philanthropy, and power relative to the monetary donation level by the donor to a nonprofit where the donor had no previous relationship.

Definitions

The definitions of key terms within this section are the variables used within this comparative quantitative analysis.

Achievement. McClelland (1961) defined achievement as an inner need, or drive used to achieve excellence. Staurowsky et al. (1996) explained achievement with the creation of success factors such as loyalty and supporting the nonprofit with both related to the success of the donor. Verner et al. (1998) also related the motive of achievement, and the factors associated with

18

loyalty to the nonprofit and the creation of tangible structures that enable the nonprofit to achieve positive results. Donors may provide a monetary donation to the basilica to seek new ways to grow the reputation, stature, and prominence of the basilica throughout the world. The study measured the achievement variable using a 5-point Likert-type scale. The variable measure attributed a numerical value by assigning numbers from one to five corresponding as 1-Strongly Disagree, 2-Disagree, 3-Neutral, 4-Agree, and 5-Strongly Agree. An ANOVA tested the means for each respective variable.

Affiliation. Affiliation is the positive feeling associated with fitting into a group and a sense of belonging to something more substantive than oneself (Strode, 2006). McClelland (1975) defined affiliation as a motive for harmonious relationships. Other literature refers to the motive in a social vein (Strode, 2006), related to participation in an event with family and friends (Billing et al., 1985), and to the friendships created with the affiliation (Staurowsky et al., 1996). Affiliation represents guests visiting the basilica on family vacations to Florida. Donors can seek affiliation with each other as a part of a unique basilica, which is a cause or a mission larger than himself or herself. A 5-point Likert-type scale measured the affiliation variable in this survey. The variable measure attributed a numerical value by assigning numbers from one to five corresponding as 1-Strongly Disagree, 2-Disagree, 3-Neutral, 4-Agree, and 5-Strongly Agree. An ANOVA tested the means for each respective variable.

Basilica. A basilica is a Roman Catholic house of worship that has been bestowed the honorific title of basilica directly from the Pope (Pontiff and worldwide leader of the Roman Catholic Church) residing in the Vatican City in Rome, Italy (E. J. McCarthy, personal communication August 22, 2009). A basilica, according to the basilica's rector used in the study, is the Pope's home away from Rome, meaning the Pope can celebrate (preside over)

Catholic Mass (a Catholic religious worship service) only in a parish church, cathedral, or shrine named a basilica (E. J. McCarthy, personal communication July 26, 2009). The Roman Catholic Church classifies nine basilicas as major basilicas and 1,582 basilicas as minor basilicas throughout the earth (E. J. McCarthy, personal communication July 26, 2009). Seven of the nine major basilicas are in Rome in addition to basilicas in Assisi, Italy and Jerusalem, Israel (E. J. McCarthy, personal communication August 22, 2009). The Roman Catholic Church classifies the basilica in this study as one of 69 minor basilicas within the United States of America.

Monetary Donation Level. The monetary donation level is the dependent variable for the study. Zikmund et al. (2009) stated that a dependent variable is a criterion explained because the dependent variable is dependent on the independent variable or variables. In the Likert-type survey, the participants self-reported the level of donation to the basilica by identifying the donation level within one of the following five categories: 1- $1-$99; 2- $100-$199; 3- $200-$299; 4- $300-$399; 5- $400 or more.

Motivation. Maslow (1943) defined motivation as the basis of inspiration and stimulus of desires within human beings to achieve an action based on fulfilling a sequence of needs. Maslow explained motivation as an inner-drive to achieve a goal to satisfy a need. Frankl (1984) believed that man's deepest desire, or motivation, is to search for meaning and purpose in an individual's life. Frankl noted that motivation is a human emotion necessary to achieve a desire or outcome.

Philanthropy. Verner, Hecht, and Fansler (1998) defined philanthropy as an individual making an active effort to promote human welfare, an act of goodwill, or offering assistance to the needy. The concept of philanthropy can be explained in multiple ways, although is summarized by serving and altruistic behaviors (Strode, 2006). Researchers correlated the motive with providing financial sustenance while generating future opportunities for success

(Strode, 2006), as well as repaying past benefits received (Mahoney, Gladden, & Funk, 2003).

Donors may provide a monetary donation to the basilica for altruistic and philanthropic reasons

to assist the poor, assist with future growth projects, or the donors believe providing a monetary

donation is an honorable behavior. A 5-point Likert-type scale measured the philanthropy

variable on the survey. The variable measure attributed a numerical value by assigning numbers

from one to five corresponding as 1-Strongly Disagree, 2-Disagree, 3-Neutral, 4-Agree, and 5-

Strongly Agree. An ANOVA tested the means for each respective variable.

Power. Staurowsky, Parkhouse, and Sachs (1996) defined power as opportunities for

one person or group of people to exert influence and control over others. Power is associated

with influence, access to decision-makers, and inside information (Strode, 2006). Donors who

support the basilica may seek to influence decisions and the direction of future basilica growth

and projects through the motivation of power. A 5-point Likert-type scale measured the power

variable. The variable measure attributed a numerical value by assigning numbers from one to

five corresponding as 1-Strongly Disagree, 2-Disagree, 3-Neutral, 4-Agree, and 5-Strongly

Agree. An ANOVA tested the means for each respective variable.

Summary

This current chapter provided background information on the role of multiple motivation

theories within philanthropy research in addition to presenting frameworks on the role of religion

in nonprofit organizations monetary development efforts. Research frameworks associated with

sales and marketing supported theoretical frameworks applied within this study. Incorporating

background of philanthropic motivational research as evidence outlined the foundation for answering the research problem as well as testing the hypothesis, which produced statistical results highlighting the significance of this study.

The purpose of this comparative quantitative study revealed the relationship between motivations of donors providing a monetary donation to a nonprofit the donor did not have a previous relationship. Data analysis from this quantitative research helped provide information to describe the personal motivations of individual donors who provided a monetary donation to a nonprofit Roman Catholic basilica in Florida. This comparative quantitative study incorporated an ANOVA to test data provided from donors who provided a monetary donation to a nonprofit where the individual donor had no previous relationship based on the four motives of achievement, affiliation, philanthropy, and power (independent variables) relative to the level of a monetary donation (dependent variable). To determine if the respective donor motives of achievement, affiliation, philanthropy, and power are significant to the monetary donation level, this study incorporated a single regression analysis. These research findings can inform multiple nonprofits in future fundraising campaign efforts, as these nonprofit organizations will have additional information on donor motivations to provide a monetary donation to their respective nonprofit.

CHAPTER 8: LITERATURE REVIEW

This quantitative study described the relationships between motivations of donors to provide a monetary donation to a nonprofit without a previous relationship with the nonprofit. Comparisons were made of personal motivations of the target population of donors who provided a monetary donation to a nonprofit Roman Catholic basilica without a previous relationship based on the donor's monetary donation level. This study incorporated Strode's (2006) survey instrument, with permission, that used multiple motivational theoretical frameworks to test donor motivations providing monetary donations to a nonprofit. This study included an analysis of four motives of achievement, affiliation, philanthropy, and power (independent variables) relative to the monetary donation level (dependent variable).

This literature review summarized the multiple theoretical frameworks in philanthropy literature within the sub-topics of philanthropy, motivation, and the influence of religion in philanthropy in explaining a donor's motivation to provide a monetary donation to a nonprofit without a previous relationship. This chapter provides research background on the conditions of donors providing monetary donations from philanthropy literature in addition to literature associated with sales and marketing to understand donor motivations. The examination of literature on customer relationship frameworks in philanthropy, motivation, and the role of religion in philanthropy will highlight frameworks associated with for-profit businesses customer relationships extending to nonprofit donor relationships.

The philanthropy section of this chapter connects the history of nonprofit endeavors in the United States. This section focuses on both the individual donor as well as the nonprofit organizations in understanding donor motivations to provide a monetary donation where the donor did not have a previous relationship. The philanthropy investigation emphasizes research literature describing how modern philanthropic organizations are operating more like for-profit businesses in understanding donor motivations to provide a monetary donation where the donor did not have a previous relationship. The motivation section underscores psychological theories of the multiple human motivational theories of altruistic helping behaviors connecting the understanding donor motivations to provide a monetary donation where the donor did not have a previous relationship. Understanding the connections between the fields of psychology and human motivation by analyzed research literature assist nonprofits understand the motivations of individuals providing monetary donations to philanthropic nonprofits. The last sub-topic section in this chapter outlines research in the examination of donor motivations in religious congregations and other religious philanthropy in understanding donor motivations to provide a monetary donation where the donor did not have a previous relationship.

This comparative quantitative research study focused on the monetary donations of individual donors provided to nonprofit organizations and not volunteerism. A definition of volunteerism is providing individual's time to a philanthropic cause or nonprofit (Schortgen, 2006). Concepts of charity and philanthropy have evolved from the original religious foundations in the United States of America as charitable almsgiving or monetary donations to the poor and needy (Schortgen, 2006). Modern philanthropic endeavors incorporate more institutional structure and organizational alignment, similar to the structure of for-profit organizations (Schortgen, 2006). In the United States of America, individual donors account for over 75% of all monetary donations provided to nonprofits each year (Henke & Fontenot, 2009). Individual donors in the United States have provided monetary donations to beneficiaries such as the needy, the poor, educational institutions, religious organizations, and political candidates

(Schortgen, 2006). Approximately 1.5 million nonprofits are competing for monetary donations from individual donors, corporations, and foundations (Henke & Fontenot, 2009).

Philanthropy is a prevalent concept within contemporary society (Schneewind, 1996). The subject of philanthropy is without a formal disciplinary field in academia or business (Schneewind, 1996). The concept of philanthropy is an ideal that communities and organizations aspire to provide tangible services and benefits to those in need (Cugliari, 2005). Cugliari (2005) stated that individuals strive for internal and external recognition because of philanthropy. The analysis of why individual donors choose to provide a monetary donation to a respective nonprofit has been the focal point of philanthropy research in the disciplines of economics, psychology, social psychology, sociology, anthropology (Sargeant & Woodliffe, 2007). Philanthropy researchers conducted further studies in the traditional business disciplines of management, sales, and marketing (Sargeant & Woodliffe, 2007).

Burton (2010) conducted research on donor motivations to provide a monetary donation, and revealed the perspectives of the participants. Burton's research allowed the nonprofit organization to understand the philanthropic environment from the donor's perspective. The analysis of philanthropy throughout this research sought to develop an understanding of the philanthropy and charity phenomenon as it relates to the motivation of donors. This research provided further evidence to the comprehension of donor motivations of providing a monetary donation the donor did not have a previous relationship with the nonprofit.

Philanthropy Literature

Understanding philanthropy, both in practice and historical significance, assisted this study by describing relationships between donor motives providing a monetary donation where the donor did not have a previous relationship with the nonprofit based on the monetary donation level. McCully (2000) offered a functional definition of philanthropy, which addressed that most

Americans are not sure of philanthropy's meaning. McCully revealed for other Americans that

philanthropy carries a negative connotation. McCully stated that negative views of philanthropy

are associated with ambiguous language rooted in unhelpful connotations, such as terms like

nonprofit and disadvantaged. Philanthropy is a fragmented field, as a lack of national leadership

keeps philanthropic executives from public prominence (Cugliari, 2005) as well as an

inconsistent motivational theoretical framework (Strode, 2006). The words charity and

philanthropy are interchangeable within literature as respectively each involves individuals

offering altruistic helping behaviors (Cugliari, 2005).

Philanthropy, defined by Feingold (1987), is charity by offering support to those in need.

High culture and causes aided through nonprofit organizations represent multiple philanthropic

fields of scholarship, art, science, religion, and music (Feingold, 1987). Applying Feingold's

definition as the basis of a reference definition, both charity and philanthropy are synonymous in

providing monetary donations to a nonprofit because of the implied support of those in need.

Cugliari (2005) stated that philanthropy focuses on the collective common good of society

whereas, charity strictly is the support of the less fortunate. Bremner (1994) clarified charity as

providing support to remove the need, suffering, the sorrow of others, if the donor understands

the individuals in need or not. Philanthropy is the prevention and correction of social and

environmental issues, the improvement of basic living conditions, and the quality of life for

people and creatures the benefactors are familiar, and where the beneficiaries do not have a

previous relationship with the benefactors (Bremner, 1994).

Focusing on charity's unique characteristic of lessening suffering with individual

attention and immediacy, Cugliari (2005) illustrated how eliciting an emotional response from individual donors initiates the motivation of providing a monetary donation. Philanthropy

requires delving into the macro issues of the causation of individual's suffering, thus determining

how best to use motivation to address the root cause of the suffering (Cugliari, 2005). Gross

(2003) stated that philanthropic behavior requires more rational reasoning and logical thinking.

Gross offered a definition that encapsulated philanthropy as the motivational aims to create an

ideal world where charity is rare because charity would be unwarranted. Cugliari (2005)

outlined the difference between charity and philanthropy in Table 1.

Table 1

Differences Between Charity and Philanthropy

Characteristic	Charity	Philanthropy
Recipient	Individuals	Large numbers of people
Goal	Alleviate suffering	Promote common good
Interaction	Donor is known	Donor is not known
Time	Present	Future
Focus	Symptoms	Root cause of problem
Action	Giving	Giving and doing
Motivation	Emotional	Rational
Source	Income/cash	Wealth/assets

Table 1 identifies the characteristics of the differences between charity and philanthropy.

The conclusions presented in the analysis of philanthropy and charity developed by Cugliari

(2005) are to alleviate suffering, a time orientation focusing on the present, treating the

symptoms, the giving behavior, emotional motivations, familiarity with the beneficiaries, and the source income. Even though large groups of individual donors provide a monetary donation to a cause, the primary focus is assisting individuals in need (Cugliari, 2005).

With an understanding of both philanthropy and charity, Karl and Katz (1987) discussed the foundational roots of philanthropy based on Judeo-Christian beliefs in the early formation of the United States of America. This understanding is critical to comprehend donor motivations to provide a monetary donation to a nonprofit organization. When American colonists first came to the North American geographic land, which eventually became the United States, the colonists formed societies based on establishing religious freedom after living with religious persecution under a monarchy in England (Karl & Katz, 1987). The United States' strong religious foundations have served as the root of philanthropy within American culture (Karl & Katz, 1987). The foundational Judeo-Christian religious traditions ingrained philanthropy into the culture of western society by way of philanthropy's importance on self-denial, providing monetary donations for the poor, and the understanding of a social conscience (Feingold, 1987). A further exploration of the role religion has on philanthropy while applying motivational theory appear later within this literature review section of this chapter.

Separate from religion, two additional important influences of American philanthropy are the tradition of mutual assistance within the community and the representative democracy form of government (Karl & Katz, 1987). To remain a true democracy, American citizens learned to cooperate for mutual benefits serving as a social framework for philanthropic ideals (Biddle, 1953). Additional philanthropic concepts that resulted from the democratic philosophy of the United States are the motive ideals of limited government, individual autonomy, and pluralism (Karl & Katz, 1987).

Boorstin (1987) identified B. Franklin as the patron saint of American philanthropy.

Franklin's philanthropic efforts providing monetary donations helped originate various civic

institutions, hospitals, the University of Pennsylvania, and a public library (Council on

Foundations, 2000). Franklin's monetary donations focused on the philanthropic benefit of

creating a common good for improving the community and providing opportunities for people to

help themselves (Council on Foundations, 2000). Franklin's motivation to engage the in

philanthropic behavior of providing monetary donations was for the public benefit with a future-

oriented vision, and helped a large numbers of citizens the diplomat did not know personally.

Franklin's altruistic behaviors reinforced the philanthropic definition offered by Gross (2003),

who stated that philanthropy is a rational act made with the notion of eliminating the root cause

of suffering and motivated by providing beneficiaries an opportunity to create a prosperous

future for those in need.

In the 19th century, industrialists J. D. Rockefeller and A. Carnegie strongly influenced

American philanthropy (Cugliari, 2005) as the individuals provided the groundwork for

nonprofits by applying frameworks associated with traditional sales and marketing. According

to Grimm (2002), the massive wealth accumulated by Rockefeller and Carnegie was so

considerable, the two philanthropic benefactors transitioned monetary donations from retail

donations to wholesale donations. Grimm indentified retail donations as personal philanthropic

appeals to provide monetary donations. Grimm illustrated wholesale donations as monetary

contributions made directly to a large umbrella organization, such as foundations that analyze the

needs then disseminate the philanthropic organization's monetary support as the umbrella

organization sees fit.

After earning such vast personal wealth, Carnegie stated that a person in the industrialist's personal economic circumstance should become a vehicle of civilization so that philanthropy becomes an instrument for humanizing civilization (Council on Foundations, 2000). Bremner (1994) explained as the modern period of philanthropy began in the United States that Rockefeller believed ideal philanthropy was not formal charity of providing a monetary donation. Research on philanthropy requires further examinations of philanthropic business models adopted in theoretical frameworks.

The President of the United States in the 1980s, R. W. Reagan, created administration policies pertaining to taxation and government spending that had a major influence on corporate philanthropy in providing monetary donations to nonprofit organizations (Wulfson, 2001). President Reagan's economic policies called Reaganomics, decreased government funding to nonprofits (Wulfson, 2001). The responsibility of providing monetary donations and organizational funding nonprofits shifted to individual donors and the private sector business (Wulfson, 2001). The Reagan policies created a venture philanthropy phenomenon defined by (Morino, 2000). This policy of venture philanthropy established nonprofits under a traditional business venture capital model (Morino, 2000). Under the venture capital model identified by Morino, philanthropists were not similar to an individual donor providing monetary donation, as the individual donor wanted direct information and personal involvement with the nonprofit. Individual donors created a new philanthropic philosophy under the model because donors wanted to be for nonprofits what capitalists are for businesses with direct personal involvement (Morino, 2000). Donors who provide a monetary donation to a nonprofit seek a relationship as funders, strategy consultants, media advisors, and recruiters (Morino, 2000).

The philanthropic venture capital model forced philanthropic nonprofit organizations to adopt traditional strategies and business practices from the for-profit business model (Whitford, 2000). New venture capital-minded nonprofit organizations implemented procedures to create effective business-minded philanthropic organizations (Whitford, 2000). Whitford (2000) reported that this new venture capital philosophy was philanthropy with an attitude. Apparent similarities between the philanthropic paradigms of new venture capital are evident in the strategy and the philosophies of Rockefeller and Carnegie in providing monetary donations to a nonprofit. Both of the philosophies embrace philanthropy as the functional method of awarding nonprofit funding, coupled with the adoption of traditional for-profit business models (Cugliari, 2005). Cugliari (2005) observed the results of monetary donations provided by individuals to nonprofits, as these donor fundraising models are associated with traditional sales and marketing.

Many individual donors provide monetary donations to nonprofits through corporate philanthropy as Love and Higgins (2007) stated that providing monetary donations to a nonprofit contributes to strong community development; therefore is not without concerns. Tangible connections between philanthropy and corporate citizenship exist; however, Love and Higgins contended the average United States citizen has limited understanding how corporate philanthropy contributes to societal development. The researchers agreed that motivations of corporate philanthropy managers represented a continuum with altruism at one end, a variety of reciprocity motivations in the middle, to total individual self-interest at the other end of the continuum (Love & Higgins, 2007).

Love and Higgins (2007) described the importance of understanding the motivations of individuals within corporate philanthropy, which can lead to intended and unintended consequences and the potential consequences can contribute to problems in community development, and ultimately with the intended nonprofit recipients (Love & Higgins, 2007). Hoffman (2008) contended that United States corporations are generous with corporate philanthropic monetary support to nonprofit organizations. Hoffman contended the corporate generosity does not represent the true spirit of nonprofit monetary donations and philanthropic support. Hoffman concluded that United States organizations were paramount in nonprofit monetary donations when compared to international organizations throughout the earth. When corporate businesses stated the specific philanthropic motivation to provide a monetary donation, both domestic and international corporations expressed the organization's ultimate motivation was promoting new employee recruitment and retention (Hoffman, 2008).

In the late 1990s, philanthropic monetary donations from individuals, corporations, and foundations increased because of the burgeoning United States economic growth (Cugliari, 2005). Economic growth encountered a dramatic decline in the early 2000s, which resulted in nonprofit contributions falling from previous monetary donation levels because of the decline of the value of the stock markets (Cugliari, 2005). The decline in the stock market and individual personal wealth during the early 2000s led to a decrease in philanthropic monetary donations by foundations and individual private donors (Anft & Wilhelm, 2002).

Because of the current economic issues and financial constraints in the United States (Durando, 2010), the philanthropic community is operating much like traditional for-profit businesses as customer relationship and marketing strategies initiatives are increasingly incorporated. Lacey (2007) stated that relationship drivers are developed to summarize crucial motivations explaining the behaviors of customers engaged in marketing relationships. The use of a customer relationship framework, used in traditional business marketing endeavors, extended to viewing individual donors as traditional customers and focusing on the customer relationships within the nonprofits. The customer relationship theory concurrently attempted to provide economic, social, and resource are theory driver variables to individual donors of a nonprofit (Lacey, 2007).

Kelly (1991) offered a contemporary operational business definition of fundraising as the purposive process of soliciting and accepting monetary donations from individuals, corporations, and foundations by a nonprofit organization. Kelly's research findings involved an extensive amount of development research in the marketing and public relations functional areas to produce successful monetary donation campaigns for nonprofits focusing on the donor as a consumer. Bendapudi et al., (1995) classified philanthropic literature as composed of three disciplines: economics, marketing, and social psychology. Bendapudi et al. stated these disciplines incorporated the nonprofit as for-profit operational model. McKinley-Floyd and Shrestha (2008) discovered that having a strategic marketing construct to connect with nonprofit donors is critical to execute successful fundraising campaigns supporting the Bendapudi et al. (1995) research. In the relationship between the donor and the benefactor of a donation, researchers and economists were predisposed to observe only the donor and evaluate the monetary donation motivation created for the donor through the monetary donation (Bendapudi et al., 1995).

Maynard (2008) expressed the term fundraising has a short-term orientation with the basic goal of receiving an immediate monetary donation from the donor. Maynard stated that philanthropy endeavors must focus on the individual and not the specific monetary donation, thus supporting the idea of creating multiple customer relationship drivers (Lacey, 2007). Maynard supported a philanthropic approach that money will follow once the commitment from the individual is secure, creating a balance between the donor and activities of the organization.

Research conducted by Prugsamatz (2010) outlined leaders of nonprofit organizations need to create work environments that motivate employees to enhance teamwork while shaping the organizations' culture to promote development performance. The nonprofit organization can achieve the development goals through monetary donations if the donor is personally committed to the mission and vision of the nonprofit through customer relationship endeavors established by the nonprofit staff (Maynard, 2008).

Thralls (2007) explained that philanthropic success is rooted in detailed plans to increase annual monetary donation programs and capital funding from individual donors, for-profit organizations, and foundations. The respective benefactor sources depend on the nonprofit employees cultivating and building relationships to appeal to new acquaintances who may become donors (Thralls, 2007). Maynard (2008) and Thralls both agreed that successful philanthropy is paramount and will be achieved by making personal contacts to attract monetary donations from individual donors, corporate philanthropy departments, foundations, and member constituents. A variety of motivations for individual donors can offer support to nonprofits, which can be uncovered with donor relationship activities (Thralls, 2007). Thralls (2007) identified donors who have a desire to make a difference (motivated by results), a philanthropic mission compatibility (aligned with operational objectives), and have a shared vision (understanding plans for the future) as the most important aspects for the nonprofit to achieve monetary donations creating donor relationships.

Within development and fundraising efforts, other literature suggested the opposite of Bendapudi et al. (1995) that marketing and business researchers cannot only focus on the recipient of the gift. On the contrary, an organization should promote the cause to obtain the most out of donor monetary donations (Bendapudi et al., 1995). An important attribute is to ensure the fundraiser, working in the traditional organizational business framework, has

knowledge of essential marketing functions such as branding, image management, and channels

of distribution (Sargent, 1999). Such expertise in marketing management assisted nonprofits in

the implementation of monetary donation development programs and capital campaigns

(Sargent, 1999). Olsen and Galimidi (2009) discovered entrepreneurial leadership is abandoning

tradition business models of informing stakeholders of financial interests instead highlighting

quality of the marketing relationship between employees and customers is the central driver of

philanthropic value supporting the research of Sargent (1999).

Guy and Patton (1984) delved further into the concept that formal marketing campaigns,

conducted by the nonprofit must advance altruistic helping behaviors to receive monetary

donations from donors. Guy and Patton identified donor motivation as the key to success for

nonprofit organizations. Modifying development strategies to market circumstances is another

critical component when developing a profitable cause-related campaign for nonprofits

organizations to maximize success in a traditional for-profit business context (Hibbert & Horne,

1996). Development professionals within nonprofit organizations must also comprehend social,

economic, and political demands as well as discover common decision-making methods

associated with altruistic behavior while operating under a successful business model (Hibbert &

Horne, 1996).

Philanthropic research, which incorporated marketing principles, suggested the chief

focus of marketing research in philanthropy should incorporate donor development or

fundraising campaigns to increase monetary donations (Kottasz, 2003). Within a study on

comprehending professional males' altruistic behaviors, Kottasz (2003) highlighted the

significance of conducting market research on specific donor demographics because of the donors' supposed monetary donation and high earning potential. Custom fitting a message to the individual donor, based on the donor's prominent motivation to provide a monetary donation, needs to become the main-focus of marketing research for fundraising campaigns (Kottasz, 2003).

The business dynamics and economics of philanthropy research have classified the variables by the individual donor that function as predictors of the charitable behavior of providing a monetary donation (Valentinov, 2008). Commonalities incorporated within the analysis of philanthropy include the nonprofit donor motivations working within a formal organizational structure. Valentinov (2008) stated that nonprofit organizations have encapsulated two types of theories highlighting secular (for-profit) market failures as well as the individual motivations to provide a monetary donation to a nonprofit. Valentinov argued the necessities of nonprofit organizations collective self-sufficiency by the limitations of the abilities of traditional for-profit commerce organizations, to satiate human needs.

Individual donor history and demographic factors have been the focus of research of donors providing a monetary donation to a nonprofit, which includes the donor's socio-demographic status (Cunningham & Cochi-Ficano, 2002). Household income levels and matching monetary donation accounts by the individual donor's employers are factors of interest to nonprofit demographers (Okunade & Berl, 1997). Factors such as economic market conditions and nonprofit distinctiveness additionally provide evidence of noticeable influences on donors providing a monetary donation to a nonprofit organization (Ehrenberg & Smith, 2001). Maynard (2008) analyzed individual donor demographic differences that predicted donor characteristics. Other variables such as donor motivations can predict donor behavior over time (Maynard, 2008).

Much attention within philanthropic literature involved the individual donor; however, evidence was present to support the donors' relationship with the nonprofits' business operations also had an effect on the nonprofit donations and monetary donations. Andreoni (2006) stated the most important rule to achieve fundraising goals is to ask potential donors to provide a monetary donation. Individuals are more willing to provide monetary donations when asked by a representative of the nonprofit (Andreoni, 2006). A maxim among nonprofit development staff and fundraisers stated that asking donor to provide a monetary donation assists in obtaining the donation. The relationships between a nonprofit organization and a donor, and the motivations of the donor to provide monetary donations to a nonprofit are rarely studied (Yuruk, 2008). Efforts to comprehend determinants of philanthropic monetary donations have focused on demographic variables, income, and the individual's personal tax benefits of providing financial donations related to the amount of nonprofit contributions (Yuruk, 2008).

Weisbord and DeScioli (2010) established detrimental effects on donor status in their study on the interest of individuals providing charitable monetary donations to nonprofits. Weisbord and DeScioli investigated motivations by comparing economic and psychological models of charitable helping behaviors where donors set conditions on the monetary donation. The Weisbord and DeScioli research, similar to Yuruk (2008), focused on the possible tax and legal policy concerns about the enforceability of donor-imposed monetary donation restrictions. The current tax law allows donors to impose restrictions on the specific use of their nonprofit monetary donation; however, donors lack legal standing to enforce their desired restrictions in court (Weisbord & DeScioli, 2010).

Weisbord and DeScioli (2010) highlighted the concerns that encompassed Rockefeller and Carnegie between true philanthropic ideals and the economic realities of legal and tax benefits. Weisbord and DeScioli stated that society desires the encouragement of philanthropy. By offering tax incentives, or limiting the use of the monetary donation by the nonprofit, the incentives pollute the genuineness of the donor's charitable intent (Weisbord & DeScioli, 2010). Weisbord and DeScioli determined that despite the intended effect, donor status did not encourage nonprofit monetary donations, which could cause a decrease in nonprofit monetary donations by the individual donor.

Researchers studied the importance of the monetary donation solicitations in philanthropy, and Schervish and Havens (1997) outlined a positive association between nonprofit appeals and the percentage of income offered by the individual donor. Bryant, Jeon-Slaughter, Kang, and Tax (2003) offered another perspective on the factors that differentiate individuals asked by nonprofits to provide a monetary donation, from potential donors not asked. Bryant, et al. argued that personal, social, cultural, and income variables addressed the reasons individuals provide a monetary donation to nonprofits compared to individuals not asked to donate.

Andreoni and Payne (2003) developed a theoretical model of philanthropy development that incorporated monetary donations solicitations by nonprofit organizations. The Andreoni and Payne model understood that individual donors do not contribute unless specifically asked to contribute monetary support. Conversely, in the most current Andreoni (2006) research, instead of focusing on the effect of fundraising efforts on individual donor's motivation to provide a monetary donation to a nonprofit, Andreoni investigated the variation in fundraising efforts when a nonprofit received a grant from the government, and concluded that fundraising efforts fail because of the perceived outside non-donor funding source.

Individual donors who are more likely to provide a monetary donation to a philanthropic cause, are the potential donors more likely receiving solicitation over non-philanthropically minded individuals (Yuruk, 2008). Yuruk (2008) supposed that individuals could overstate the relationship between solicitation and the respective altruistic behaviors in conducting valid research. The Yuruk findings could be counter-intuitive as Barnes (2006) appealed to a phenomenon called donor fatigue. Barnes stated that fundraisers reported donor fatigue is a phenomenon where donors no longer provide a monetary donation because they become weary after receiving a wealth of different appeals for philanthropic monetary support. Donor fatigue can also explain why donors are providing less monetary donations in a fragile economy (Arcieri, 2009). Yuruk warned not to underestimate the effect of solicitation on providing a monetary donation because the ideal individual donors frequently asked to provide a monetary donation, are individuals who will likely suffer from donor fatigue, eventually becoming less prone to donate. The results match the findings of Barnes (2006) on motivation influencing donor fatigue.

Yuruk (2008) discovered individual female donors are more generous than males. Miller (2008) revealed females were motivated by a professional personal connection, a need, or because it was a right behavior to engage. However, Yen (2002) illustrated that gender does not have a noteworthy effect on philanthropic monetary donations. Regardless of gender, researchers did not focus on the effect of the nonprofit's employees on philanthropic behavior (Yuruk, 2008). Further evidence supported that fundraising endeavors by the nonprofit were vital in increasing both the propensity to give and the level of monetary donations from individual donors (Yuruk, 2008). If the donors were male or female, connections to the nonprofit existed in the donor's opinion of the nonprofit business operations (Yuruk, 2008).

Khanna, Posnett, and Sandler (1995), along with additional research supported by Okten and Weisbrod (2000), demonstrated positive relationships existed between charitable contributions collected by a nonprofit and fundraising expenses accrued by the nonprofit. Khanna et al. and Okten and Weisbrod researched tax-return data from nonprofits and illustrated a positive relationship between a nonprofit's expenses and the total monetary contributions received. Similar relationships in research conducted by both Schervish and Havens (1997) and Yuruk (2008), using survey data from a smaller sample additionally supported the relationships.

Yuruk (2008) criticized nonprofits for spending too many resources on direct fundraising endeavors. Nonprofits' focus on development costs became so intense, many nonprofit auditors and potential donors scrutinized the expenses and indicated that fundraising expenditures should be the principal characteristic evaluated when estimating the quality of nonprofit organizations (Yuruk, 2008). Research conducted by Yuruk provided evidence that excessive fundraising expenses are legitimate.

Lackie (2010) demonstrated non-donors should become the focus of development efforts as they are the most likely, when compared to current donors, to change their behavior. With the correct motivation non-donors, who share similar demographic characteristics with current donors, could provide a monetary donation (Lackie, 2010). However, data on nonprofit organizations supported that average nonprofits spent around 18% of total philanthropic monetary contributions on donor fundraising expenses compared to the nonprofit industry's peer reviewed accepted standard of 10% (Bradley, Jansen, & Silverman, 2003). Jacobs and Marudas (2006) estimated from research that nonprofit organizations spent too much money on fundraising expenses. Jacobs and Marudas investigated 76 nonprofit organizations and revealed 24 of the 76 engaged in excessive fundraising expenses.

The most recent studies on the motivations of donors revealed results based on the identification of specific donors or a specific nonprofit. Gaulke (2010) conducted research to test the motivations of first-time online donors. A significant statistical relationship between current and first-time donors examined the online donor motivation of a small nonprofit parent-of-preschoolers group in Wisconsin based on behavior models (Gaulke, 2010). The dedication and accomplishments of the nonprofit organization had positive response relationships from the participants as the main motivation to provide a monetary donation (Gaulke, 2010).

Burton (2010) applied attribution theory to test the motivations of professional football athletes, which provided evidence for nonprofits, reinforcing the importance of traditional for-profit customer relationship with their donors. Attribution theory explained how individuals interpret events relating directly to their thinking and behavior to provide a monetary donation (Burton, 2010). Burton demonstrated that participants' perspectives permitted the nonprofit to understand the environment from the donors' frames of reference to solicit a monetary donation.

Motivation Literature

Understanding human motivation, both in philanthropic practice as well as historical human theoretical development, assist the explorations of relationships of donor motives providing a monetary donation where the donor did not have a previous relationship with the nonprofit. Henke and Fontenot (2009) discussed the positive emotions that emerge within the individual donor while providing a monetary donation. The motivations of donors were a considerable predictor of providing monetary donations to nonprofits, particularly when donors supported children and elderly causes (Henke and Fontenot, 2009). Alternately, a sense of community service and pride were the major predictors when donors provided monetary donations to offer medical support for the poor, assisted low-income individuals who receive employment, or fostered teens' community involvement (Henke & Fontenot, 2009). Fundraising efforts for nonprofits gained an advantage when nonprofit monetary donation appeals based on the understanding of individual donor motivations for providing monetary donation to nonprofit causes (Henke & Fontenot, 2009). The examination of literature on human motivation demonstrated how motivation influenced donors and nonprofits having a traditional customer and for-profit business relationship in which the relationships of donor's motivations used for development campaigns to increase monetary donations.

Teraji (2009) stated that individuals have a range of possible individual selves, as the researcher offered an economic model of how the motivations of intentional self-change transpire within an individual. The personal human motivations within the self-system are comprehensive and dynamic as diverse self-representations activate, depending on the personal individual circumstances (Teraji, 2009). Evaluation among the self and the ideal self have imperative motivational consequences as the reaction to apparent inconsistency can be fashioned toward the desired motivational change, manipulated by forces such as a nonprofit organization soliciting monetary donations from donors (Teraji, 2009).

Teraji (2009) explained that self-verification is also an important factor in the individual's motivational system used by nonprofit organizations to ascertain individual donor motivations in providing a monetary donation. Teraji's self-verification concept challenged the intentional self-change ideal, as individuals may have personal static internal areas, where there are no attempts or motivations toward self-change (Teraji, 2009). The Teraji postulate illustrated how optimal and sub-optimal economic outcomes occur as emotions and motivations by nonprofits to understand and meet the various needs of individual donors.

Maslow's (1943) hierarchy of needs illustrated one of the foremost philosophies on human motivation in psychology. According to the theory offered by Maslow, humans motivate by a series of needs, and basic human needs are satisfied before an individual will seek a higher order need (Maslow, 1943). The lowest need in Maslow's theoretical framework is physiological, which includes essential human nourishment such as hunger and thirst. An individual must satisfy the safety and security need, which follows the physiological need, before seeking the next highest need as expressed by Maslow. The final three needs contained in Maslow's theory demonstrated the commitment for growth, belongingness/love needs, esteem needs, and finally self-actualization, which all build to an advanced stage of development for humans. Figure 1 outlines Maslow's theoretical framework below.

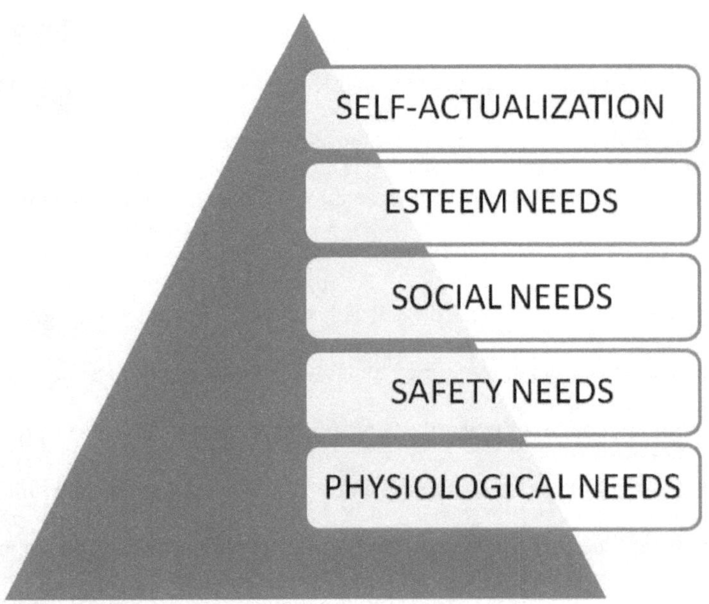

Figure 1. Maslow's Hierarchy of Human Needs Theory (Source: Maslow, 1943).

The belongingness stage illustrates the aspiration of acceptance in a group, which can be in a social structure or an intimate relationship, whereas in the esteem stage a person seeks recognition and achievement. The seldom-achieved ultimate need is self-actualization, in which Maslow (1943) made the case that humans can strive for the ideal goal. Living at the self-actualization stage entails self-fulfillment, meaning humans experience a sense of complete and

ultimate satisfaction (Maslow, 2009).

Maslow's (1943) hierarchy of needs offered a basis for understanding human motivation.

Maslow's theory used within philanthropy was a model to describe an altruistic helping behavior

within Strode's (2006) research. Maslow's theory of human motivation analyzed motivation

incorporating an altruistic helping behavior (Strode, 2006). Donors who fulfilled needs based on

Maslow's theory incorporated the three growth needs as a reason to provide a monetary

donation, which is principle when seeking to understand motivations effect on providing a

monetary donation to a nonprofit. Belongingness and love needs connect precisely to the social

motive derivative from Billing et al. (1985), while the esteem needs explained multiple motives,

including power, special treatment, access to private information, and public recognition (Verner

et al., 1998).

The highest of Maslow's (1943) needs, self-actualization, illustrated the motive of

philanthropy. The theory of altruism, as defined by Gray (1994) is a pattern of behavior related

to helping another without thought of reward, a behavior that occurs when donors provide a

monetary donation to a nonprofit. Gray's explanation of altruism corresponded with the pinnacle

of Maslow's model, where the scenario was possible for an individual to achieve complete

satisfaction through selfless acts (1943). Strode (2006) argued there is no true notion of altruism,

as an individual would donate to achieve a higher level of satisfaction, which can be viewed as a

selfish act. In analysis of altruism as a helping behavior, Maslow's needs theory apply to the

literature in philanthropy and provided a theoretical comprehension of empirical evidence of

providing a monetary donation where the donor did not have a previous relationship with a

nonprofit.

Not all researchers agreed with Maslow's philosophy that self-actualization was the ultimate determinant on human motivation and development. Rennie (2008) explained that Maslow could have increased his efforts to defend the veracity of the formulation of a need within the hierarchy. Rennie illustrated that Maslow could have offered tangible specifics, which would have signified the satisfaction of higher needs were reliant on the lower needs first being satisfied.

Maslow encountered resistance in the psychology field conversely stating that self-actualization is the ultimate motivation governing human behavior as the lower needs were irrelevant to achieving self-actualization (Rennie, 2008). Maslow allowed the postulate to go unchallenged because of the rhetorical power the theory offered the humanistic psychological movement (Rennie, 2008). Because self-actualization was such an esteemed philosophical human motivator, the issue became the chief human motivation and was resilient through disputes, even though some researchers stated that individuals are principally motivated to satisfy security needs (Rennie, 2008).

Another theory in the analysis of human motivation incorporated by Staurowsky et al. (1996) explained donor motives in providing monetary donations in the paradigm of human motivation, developed by Birch and Veroff (1966). The Birch and Veroff theory concentrated on understanding what makes human beings act through research that involved a series of discerning incentive systems to motivate individuals. A person's behavior is goal-oriented and motivated by consumption (Birch & Veroff, 1966).

The researchers created seven exclusive incentive systems that described all possible human motivations (Birch & Veroff, 1966). Birch and Veroff described sensory, curiosity, and achievement as social incentive systems, as the motivations did not rely on the influence of others. Birch and Veroff identified the last three as affiliation, aggression, power, and independence as social systems. Some of these motivational systems identified by Birch and Veroff were included in this study in addition to the Strode (2006) research.

Birch and Veroff (1966) articulated the sensory incentive system based on the human senses of tasting, seeing, hearing, smelling, and feeling as motivators. The avoidance of pain was the key human motivator in the Birch and Veroff system. The Birch and Veroff curiosity incentive system, entailed changes in stimulation desires to experience a feeling based on an intrinsic curiosity (Strode, 2006). The final social incentive system, which focused on achievement, referred to the need to achieve success in contests or competitions using a superficial set of standards (Birch & Veroff, 1966).

The first of Birch and Veroff's (1966) social incentive system was the affiliation motive. An affiliation motivation is the drive for humans to assemble with similar individuals (Birch & Veroff, 1966). The individual human fear rejection and isolation, as the attributes damage the motivation of affiliation (Strode, 2006). The aggressive incentive system focused on the instinct of humans to act in an aggressive manner, purposefully injuring another for explanations include various responses from frustration to protection (Birch & Veroff, 1966). Power, described by Birch and Veroff, is the motivation for humans to exert influence over the individual's environment. The final social motive offered by Birch and Veroff was independence, which recognized the motivation to accomplish a task without the help of others.

Birch and Veroff's (1966) paradigm of human motivation provided an extensive theoretical review of the influential motivations that explain the drive of actions within human psychology. The Birch and Veroff research is applicable to multiple disciplines because the paradigm's ability to illustrate the described incentive systems overlaps. Motivational actions describe a multitude of donor factors and behaviors presented by Strode (2006).

Incorporating the ideas set forth by Birch and Veroff (1966), a human could be motivated to attend a religious house of worship based on curiosity of gaining new spiritual knowledge. However, power influences individuals associated with attending a large house of worship influential in a respective community, such as a basilica. The Birch and Veroff theory assisted in understanding donor motivation, as Staurowsky et al. (1996) demonstrated when an investigation multiple incentive systems as motivations for altruistic helping behaviors. The social motive relates to the affiliation incentive system as described by Birch and Veroff with the power incentive system implemented directly from the paradigm (Strode, 2006).

Research conducted by Strode (2006) revealed the Birch and Veroff (1966) theory did not identify an altruistic helping behavior as a human motivation. The motivation of philanthropy preserved in every instrument question, implies an individual is motivated to donate based on the concept of not receiving anything in return (Strode, 2006). Birch and Veroff's research on motivation combined experimental research observations of humans.

A popular theory within motivation research is the social cognitive theory applied to numerous fields of research. The social cognitive theory, based on the research of Bandura (1986), formulated around human motivation as a function of the proactive nature of individuals. The social cognitive theory was a derivative of the social learning theory (Bandura, 1986). Human motivation, as theorized by Bandura, is an interaction between three influences. Bandura explained an individual's behavior affects personal factors, environmental factors, and a responsive human's behavior (Strode, 2006). Bandura identified the interaction of human behavior as triadic reciprocality. Triadic reciprocality explained how internal factors, unique to individuals based upon external factors from their environment, ultimately leading to behavior

(Strode, 2006). The triadic reciprocality relationship theorized by Bandura is illustrated in

Figure 2 below.

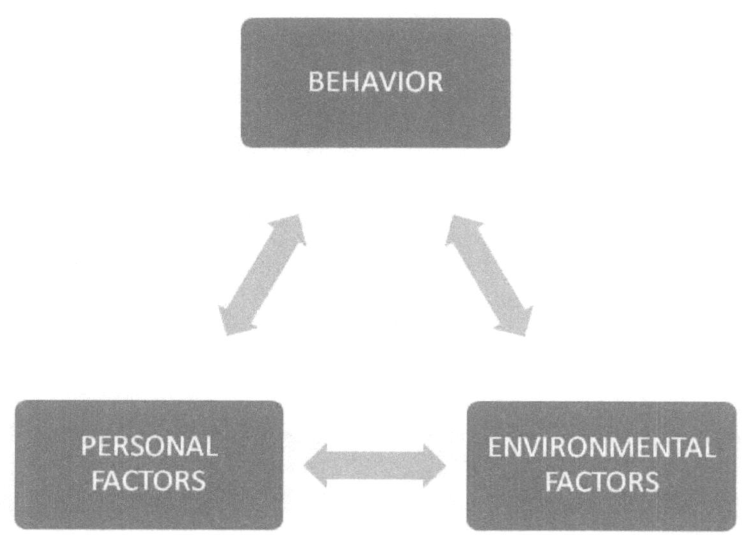

Figure 2. Bandura's Triadic Recriprocality Theory (Source: Bandura, 1986).

Personal factors within the relationship include a multitude of internal processes,

including cognitive, affective, and biological events that influence an individual (Bandura,

1986). Environmental aspects refer how an individual's surroundings help determine both

behavior and temperament (Bandura, 1986). The social cognitive theory is unique because of the

circular relationship of the factors (Strode, 2006). Conversely, a one-way model is used when

the personal factors and environmental factors combine to influence behavior has an impact on

altering personal and environmental factors in a similar manner (Bandura, 1986).

Strode (2006) illustrated another motivational theory used to understand human

motivations with the Herzberg's motivation-hygiene theory (Herzberg, Mausner, & Snyderman,

1959). The theory applies to highlight job satisfaction but can also explain human motivations in donors providing a monetary donation to a nonprofit. Herzberg, Mausner, and Snyderman stated certain factors exist in the cause satisfaction, as another distinct set of factors cause dissatisfaction. Herzberg's motivation-hygiene theory theorized that satisfaction and dissatisfaction act independently of each other.

As expressed by Chelladurai (1999), motivators lead to satisfaction, while dissatisfaction is associated with hygiene factors. For an individual to achieve high job satisfaction, motivational factors such as achievement, responsibility, the ability to grow professionally, and the appeal of the specific job lead to high satisfaction (Chelladurai, 1999). However, Chelladurai explained that particular hygiene factors must be present for an employee to experience dissatisfaction with the job. Hygiene factors have included procedures of the organization, job conditions, security, and distributive factors (Chelladurai, 1999). Figure 3 illustrates Herzberg's motivation-hygiene theory below.

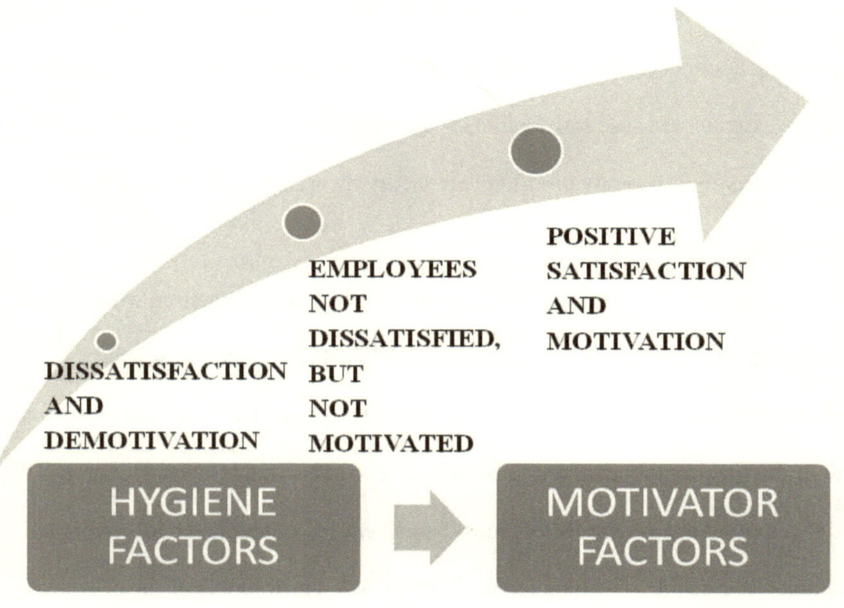

Figure 3. Herzberg's Motivation Hygiene (Two-Factor) Theory (Source: Herzberg, 1959).

Connections exist among the motivation-hygiene theory and Maslow's hierarchy of needs, as the lower level needs in Maslow's (1943) theory are germane to the hygiene factors linked with Herzberg's (1959) Motivation-Hygiene Theory. For an individual to achieve higher-level needs, one must meet particular lower-level needs or hygiene factors before an individual is compelled to ascend to higher needs (Strode, 2006). The concepts are applicable in understanding donor behavior to provide monetary donations to nonprofits, as the concepts achieve lower level needs and hygiene factors before an individual is motivated to engage in philanthropy (Strode, 2006).

Incorporating Herzberg's (1959) theory, individuals were motivated to donate based on remuneration that served as motivators for the behavior (Strode, 2006). Classified as success factors and recognized by Staurowsky et al. (1996) and Mahony et al. (2003), like the need for achievement. Achievement rewards served as an impetus for contentment while employing

Herzberg's theory (Strode, 2006). Herzberg's theory described individual job satisfaction within

an organization; however, the theory's applicability extends to the motivations of individual

donor behavior within literature and Maslow's (1943) hierarchy of needs theory in Figure 4

below.

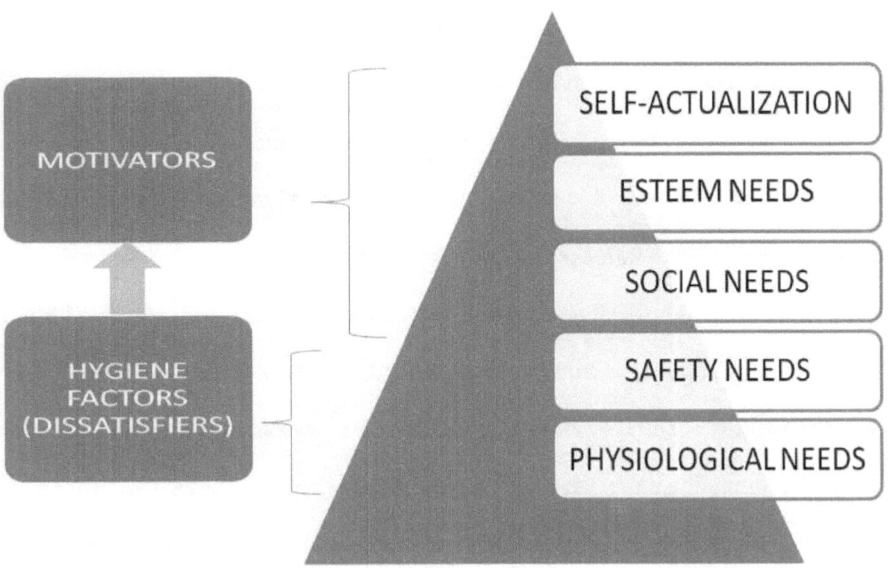

Figure 4. Motivation: Maslow's Needs and Herzberg's Hygiene Theory (Source: Maslow, 2009 and Herzberg, 1959).

This research includes analysis that measured variables by incorporating McClelland's

(1961) theory of needs, identified in motivation research as the learned needs theory.

McClelland offered the needs as motivators for human behavior applied to individual donors

within the research (Strode, 2006). The study used a quantitative Likert-type scale developed by

Strode for measuring the underlying psychosocial motives behind donors providing a monetary

donation, based on McClelland's theory of needs, in addition to the altruistic helping motive of

philanthropy.

The postulate of McClelland's (1961) theory described individual motivations as three specific needs of achievement, affiliation, and power (Strode, 2006). Achievement was the first need identified by McClelland, which explained the motivation to achieve success. Individuals motivated by the need to achieve will reject low-risk situations because the accomplishment achieved seems less worthy. However, while individuals avoid high-risk situations when achieving success, consider success fortunate providence (McClelland, 1961).

McClelland's (1961) second need of affiliation advocated that individuals sought peaceful relationships and conformed to standards to attain acceptance. McClelland described the final need of power in two separate manners. The first was an individual who searched for personal power, then wished to influence others (McClelland, 1975). The other sought institutional power, which is a social power more goal-oriented, for an organization and is mostly concerned with unity as opposed to authority (McClelland, 1975). McClelland's (1961) theory of needs was an analysis tool used in workplace motivation as well as applied to the motives identified in philanthropy literature. As evident in the Strode (2006) research, McClelland's (1961) theory of needs afforded new theoretical ideals and motivation within philanthropic literature. McClelland (1961) identified the hallmark motives. McClelland categorized under each of the three needs of affiliation, achievement, and power, and collectively provided a proven theory for the basis of the research.

To provide support to McClelland's theory (1961), Mahony, Gladden, and Funk (2003) stated the donor related the motivation of achievement to personal achievements. Assumptions that an individual who donated to a nonprofit had a basic desire for the nonprofit to succeed, provided the donor a sense of satisfaction based on the organization's achievements (Mahony et al., 2003). Affiliation assumed the satisfaction of providing to a nonprofit is a desire to affiliate and belong with a particular group (Verner, Hecht, & Fansler, 1998). Categorizing philanthropy under affiliation assumed the satisfaction of providing opportunities to other individuals be deemed a sense of wishing to belong and become affiliated with the group (Strode, 2006). The motive of power showed that egotism appeared by wanting recognition and acknowledgement for contributions (McClelland, 1972).

As Strode (2006) created and validated the survey instrument in this study, Strode made the assertion to pair McClelland's (1961) theory of needs with a combination of the factors in previously developed instruments and donor motivation research to provide sound theory to the motives identified empirically in earlier studies. The implications of these studies along with the data revealed from the Strode (2006) survey instrument will demonstrate donor motivations to donate monetary support to a nonprofit where there is no previous relationship with the donor and nonprofit. Additional research conducted on motivation and donor philanthropy occurred since the Strode research.

A more recent analysis of egalitarian motives in humans offered important motivational factors underlying the evolution of a strong bond of reciprocity and cooperation (Dawes, Fowler, Johnson, McElreath, & Smirnov, 2007). Participants in laboratory games willingly altered other participants' incomes at a detrimental cost to themselves because participants thought that it was the right thing to do (Dawes et al., 2007). This result applies to the understanding of why individuals to provide a monetary donation to a nonprofit without previous relationship with the donor based on the philanthropic motivation because it is a right and benevolent. Dawes et al. observed the effect of promoting cooperation among the participants and observed the phenomenon sacrificing a self-benefit to be an altruistic helping behavior. The researchers were still unsure about the cause of the altruistic helping behavior although postulated that punishment and reward intended at fostering cooperation is indistinguishable from efforts to generate

equality (Dawes et al., 2007).

Conducting an experimental game that isolated egalitarian motives, resulted from the

research and illustrated that participants expanded and reduced other participants' incomes at a

personal cost, although no cooperative behavior was being reinforced, which can explain the

motivation for an altruistic helping behavior (Dawes et al., 2007). However, the researchers

noted that emotions directed at top earners became progressively more negative as inequality

increased in the experimental game (Dawes et al., 2007). Participants who expressed the

emotions spent more to reduce above-average earners' incomes and to increase below-average

earners' incomes that contribute to understanding donor motivations in providing to those in need

(Dawes et al., 2007). The results suggested that egalitarian motives affect income-altering

behaviors as applied to understanding motivations donating to a nonprofit where the donors had

no previous relationship and knowledge of the situation, much as the participants used in the

experimental game conducted by Dawes et al. (2007).

Olivola (2009) conducted a study on human motivation directly applied to philanthropy.

The researcher established individuals search for positive experiences and avoid negative

experiences (Olivola, 2009). Evidence involving human motivations as well as philanthropic

helping behaviors, consider pain and effort to be deterrents, meaning that understanding a

difficult chore will be painful and effortful will decrease the motivation to perform the task

(Olivola, 2009). Research experiments conducted by Olivola discovered individuals' willingness

to provide a monetary donation to a nonprofit cause increases when the contribution process

expects to be a painful effort in contrast to an easy and enjoyable nonprofit contribution effort.

Olivola called this phenomenon the martyrdom effect to explain how the idea of suffering for a cause leads individuals to attribute more worth to future philanthropic contributions, earning more funds for the nonprofit and an emotion of self-satisfaction for the individual donor.

Olivola (2009) contended the martyrdom effect helps to explain the Liu and Aaker (2008) study that revealed a donor's willingness to donate increased if the individual first thought about volunteering time to the nonprofit. Olivola postulated that volunteering involved exerting effort, along with surrendering personal time, as the phenomenon suggests a manifestation of the martyrdom effect. However, detrimental to the nonprofit organization, Liu and Aaker conversely demonstrated a donor's willingness to donate decreased if potential individual donors first thought about donating money instead of volunteering time.

Olivola (2009) stated that results uncovered by Liu and Aaker (2008) are consistent with the martyrdom effect, as contemplating providing a monetary donation moves individuals to consider various ways of contributing, which includes means involving some amount of pain-effort. Having individual donors focus exclusively on monetary donations leads the individuals to spend less time considering other ways of contributing, along with potential contributions involving a pain-effort (Olivola, 2009). The martyrdom effect predicted that individuals would consider the contributions less meaningful and contribute less if the individuals provided a monetary donation and there was no pain-effort (Olivola, 2009).

Olivola (2009) contended that consideration of the martyrdom effect for implementation at nonprofit fundraising events. Incorporating basic human psychology in philanthropic endeavors assumes that individuals are motivated to avoid pain and effort, thus making the fundraising experience as easy and enjoyable as possible to attract more participants to provide a monetary donation to a nonprofit organization (Olivola, 2009). The results discovered by

Olivola presented philanthropic success is challenging as the participants are more likely to provide a monetary donation to nonprofit efforts and tasks.

Olivola (2009) stated that challenging donors will contribute to the success of a nonprofit fundraiser but conversely, painful-effortful fundraising events are inefficient ways of philanthropic development. Olivola maintained an existence between motivating donors with a challenge and a forceful, possible pain-influenced, motivation. A relevant study conducted by Charity Navigator (2007) revealed in 2007, special event fundraisers (including painful-effortful fundraising events) cost nonprofits $1.33 for every $1 donated, compared to the nonprofit organizational average of $0.13 for every $1 received (Olivola, 2009). Within the Charity Navigator study, just 15% of the nonprofits benefited from hosting special events rather than traditional philanthropic development activities such as asking for a monetary donation (Olivola, 2009).

Religion in Philanthropy Literature

The following section of this literature review is an analysis of specific theories regarding the relationship of religion and the motivations of altruistic helping behaviors, in addition to religion's historical influence on providing a monetary donation to a nonprofit organization. Understanding religion's influence on philanthropy assists this study by describing the relationship between donor motives of providing a monetary donation where the donor did not have a previous relationship with the nonprofit. The following section includes donors providing monetary donations to religious nonprofit organizations, religion's influence on philanthropy, and religion's influence on human motivation to engage in altruistic helping behaviors. Available literature on the topic of religion within philanthropy provided evidence regarding the influence of religious beliefs on motivating donors to provide a monetary donation to nonprofits.

The research in this study presents new knowledge to the business and philanthropic development fields, as no study has attempted to describe donor motivation of providing monetary donations to a religious nonprofit with no previous relationship with the donor. The examination of literature about religion's influence on philanthropy demonstrated how religion affects donors and nonprofits in which there are established relationships between donors and motivations to provide a monetary donation to a religious nonprofit.

The foundation of charitable behaviors in the United States has roots in organized religion although ample evidence of religious ideals are evident in the general sector as well (Shortgen, 2006). Literature within religious philanthropy included a study by Johnston (2002) who stated that satisfaction of donors providing a monetary donation to a religious nonprofit incorporated multiple motivations for the donor. The motivations included advancing the kingdom of God, gaining a sense of warmth and fulfillment from seeing the fruitfulness of the organization's work, and a personal sense of meaning and significance gained through the donors' participation creating a sense of hope for the future (Johnston, 2002).

Bremner (1996) stated the three major monotheistic religions of Judaism, Christianity, and Islam charity endorse providing monetary donations to nonprofits. Each of the three promotes charity as an obligation, offering a strong human motivator to provide monetary donations (Bremner, 1996). Bremner supported that strong religious foundations are essential to understanding American philanthropy. The Jewish Torah and Christian Old Testament teaches if a needy person is among you, do not harden your heart and shut your hand against your needy fellow man (Deuteronomy 15:7-11). Christians trained in charitable philosophy know that philanthropy is encouraged in the parable of the Good Samaritan, as many Christian denominations require a specific tithe, commonly encouraged as 10% of an individual's annual income (Bremner, 1996). A righteous man, promoted by the religion of Islam according to the Qur'an, is defined as an individual for the love of Allah (God) gives one's wealth to one's kinsfolk, to the orphans, to the needy (Quar'an Sura 2:177).

Maimonides, a Jewish Rabbi and philosopher, offered levels of charitable giving, or a specific code in part of his seminal writings contained in the Torah (Ott, 2001). Maimonides' code was one of the earliest recorded attempts to identify degrees of goodness in providing charity, thus articulating a theory of providing monetary donations (Ott, 2001). Maimonides theorized guaranteeing a home in the afterlife (or heaven) was the prime motivator for charitable offerings that individuals serving food and drink to poor men and orphans, will receive an answer when calling to God and find delight in the answer received (Maimondies, 1979).

Winthrop (1630), in an early American sermon, recognized a promise between the Puritans (a Christian religious denomination comprising of original America colonists) and God that required people living within a Christian society to offer assistance to those in need. Winthrop explained the relationship between the colonial wealthy and poor having stated the rich, and the strong should not eat up the poor, nor should the poor and despised rise up against superiors and shake off personal yoke (Winthrop, 1630). Instead, Winthrop (1630) proposed that every man reside in a bond of brotherly love whereby service and riches honor the Lord.

The role of religion is pertinent when discussing the propensity of individual donors to provide a monetary support to a nonprofit in this study. Definitions signifying religious philanthropy are critical for the analysis respective of the perception of the religion of individual donors providing monetary donations to a nonprofit. This comparative quantitative research study included a Roman Catholic basilica where the donors provided a monetary donation within the past calendar year. An assumption maintains that most participants are members of the

Roman Catholic faith in parochial dioceses within the participants' respective hometowns. However, to apply the study of providing monetary donations where the donor did not have a previous relationship with the nonprofit, the influence of religion needs to be an aspect of the significance of this analysis. An individual donor may identify religion as a belief in a higher power (Shortgen, 2006). Other individual donors may consider themselves religious only when active in a formal religion or congregation (Shortgen, 2006).

Sullivan (1985) examined church contributions and attendance using 1983 survey data from more than 2,000 Californian Protestants for an economic study. Sullivan's framework of simultaneous equations sought to alleviate afterlife challenges with the conjecture charitable service applied posthumously, in addition to the control for the pressure of increasing age on contributions. Sullivan discovered providing monetary donations and church attendance rose with income and age. Sullivan connected people's belief in the necessity of tithing to improved monetary donations. Incorporating tithing increased the weekly contributions by about $2 for women (about 33%) and significantly more ($2.70 or 37%) for men, (Sullivan, 1985).

Sullivan's (1985) findings are contrary to Bremner (1996), who defined charity as providing monetary support or service to remove the suffering and sorrow of others even if those in need are known to the donor or not. Ziliak (2004) stated that charity and philanthropy connected to passionate fixations on deep personal and meaningful ideals. Despite the aims of philanthropists to compel donors by sharing the intentions of an ideal society, philanthropy entailed reciprocity among the benefactors and the beneficiaries (Ziliak, 2004). Ziliak revealed religious and philanthropic experiences were intensely obvious as philanthropists felt empowerment and identification from nonprofit activities. Additionally, the domestic American hybrid of public, private, and nonprofit agencies serving the people vacillates without the

assistance of international cultural and religious philanthropic perspectives (Ziliak, 2004).

Researchers have not revealed that personal religion is associated with a motivation to

help others, which includes providing a monetary donation to a nonprofit (Shortgen, 2006).

However, Friedrichs (1960) stated that a religious belief in God associated positively with self-

reported charitable actions. A departure from Friedrichs' (1960) research was Allport (1966)

who stated philanthropic behavior is complex respective to the range of ways in which an

individual donor may be considered religious. Altruism aligns with caring for others more than

practical religious behavior based on individual donors self-reports within a study (Tate &

Miller, 1971). Anft and Lipman (2003) discovered religious nonprofits had a considerable

influence on donations. Houses of worship or other religious causes received more than three of

every four philanthropic dollars donated by Americans earning $50,000 or more annually (Anft

& Lipman, 2003).

Steinberg and Wilhelm (2003) examined religious versus non-religious monetary

donations from individual donors and discovered that 21% of respondents claiming no personal

religion contributed to religious organizations. Assumptions were necessary in evaluating

donors from Steinberg and Wilhelm's study in providing a monetary donation to a religiously

affiliated nonprofit, as respondents were limited only to heads of households. Religious

affiliation did positively affect charitable monetary donations according to Steinberg and

Wilhelm. Steinberg and Wilhelm illustrated that religion appeared to assimilate to non-religious

monetary donation, as individual donors acknowledging any religion are more likely to make a

monetary donation and additionally make larger monetary donations than individual donors with

no acknowledgement of religion.

Having religious beliefs maintained a vital role in motivation and donor philanthropy (Cascione, 2000). The religious ideal is the basis for the Ahlberg (1996) study that examined motives of monetary donations of a wealthy congregation to a Christian church in the United States. Ahlberg demonstrated the majority of church members in one independent congregation provided monetary donations to nonprofits that benefited the donor directly, as other donors provided a monetary donation to serve those considered less fortunate and in most need of support. Schortgen (2006) revealed older, white, well-educated, male Protestants (non-Catholic Christians) led households, are most likely to provide significant monetary donations to nonprofit organizations.

Research conducted by Locke (2002) established a relationship between Frankl's (1984) self-transcendence theory and Maslow's (1943) self-actualization theory. Frankl (1984), a Jewish survivor of Nazi concentration camps in World War II, believed that a human's deepest desire and motivation in life is to search for meaning and purpose. Locke explained how the relationship affected philanthropic motivations within the church, as the spiritual dimension of motivational theory explored in the study's analysis. Locke maintained the way the church (the collective faith or Christian denomination) applied to motivational theory from Maslow's hierarchy of needs, represents an incomplete scope of motivational theory to provide a monetary donation to a nonprofit.

Suffering, self-sacrifice, and taking a stand toward conditions are the basic human motivations (Locke, 2002). Locke's research supposed that motivation was more than merely alleviating suffering, as service in the church provided more meaning in life than only weekly church attendance. Locke incorporated the principles and motivations toward providing a monetary donation to support philanthropic church endeavors.

Peifer (2010) discovered that religion-based monetary donations are based on complex human motivations. Donors with religious and economic motives are often competing in opposing directions when providing a monetary donation (Peifer, 2010). Assumptions are made that monetary donations from individual donors are not know to the congregation, Peifer (2010) stated that God is always watching and donors take this into account when providing to a religious nonprofit. Choosing whether to provide monetary donations is an economic decision by the donor, thus a rational choice is considered by the donor. Peifer (2010) discovered an ecumenical approach to explaining religion whereas this theoretical approach should be considered when examining the religious and economic conditions for religious-based nonprofit donors.

Summary

This chapter included explorations of literature in philanthropy, motivation, and religion in philanthropy. By understanding philanthropy, human motivation, and religion's role in philanthropy, related to altruistic helping behaviors in practice and historical significance, this literature review assisted the description of relationships between motives of donors providing a monetary donation to a nonprofit when the donor did not have a previous relationship with the nonprofit based on the monetary donation level. The multiple theoretical frameworks used for this comparative quantitative research examined the phenomenon of providing monetary donations from literature associated with sales and marketing, in addition to human motivation theory. The examination of literature on customer relationship frameworks in philanthropy, motivation, and the role of religion in philanthropy, provided evidence how these sub-topics, associated with traditional business marketing activities, extend to donors and nonprofits having a traditional customer and for-profit business relationship while appealing to donor's altruistic motivations.

The philanthropy section included analysis of the history of philanthropy in the United States as literature that focused on both the individual donor as well as the philosophical understanding of nonprofit organizations, highlighted research regarding many ways modern philanthropy organizations operate like traditional businesses. Understanding that philanthropy assimilates theoretical frameworks associated with sales and marketing is important to describe motivational theories of donors providing monetary donations to a nonprofit. The motivation section outlined the psychological understanding of human motivation and altruistic helping behaviors using multiple motivational theory frameworks. Analyzed research in the psychology field of human motivation and the parallels to philanthropy create an understanding of why individuals provide monetary donations to a nonprofit organization. The religion in philanthropy section outlined behaviors leading donors to provide monetary donations within religious contexts. The section highlighted recent research in the analysis of donor motivations in religious congregations and nonprofit organizations.

General philanthropy research included in this chapter incorporated sales and marketing frameworks by nonprofit development personnel with research conducted by Lacey (2007) and Yuruk (2008). Both Maslow (1943) and McClelland (1975) explained motivation theory, relating how the researchers' respective theories directly applied human motivation to donors providing a monetary donation to a nonprofit. Based theoretically on McClelland's theory of needs, Strode (2006) created the survey instrument used with permission in this study. The section covering philanthropy in religion maintained theoretical frameworks based on research from Locke (2002) by incorporating motivational theories from Maslow and Frankl (1984). The theory that God is watching when a donor provides a monetary donation offers a motivation for donors to provide a monetary donation to a religious nonprofit (Peifer, 2010).

The synthesis of philanthropy, human motivation, and religion's role in philanthropy, related to altruistic helping behaviors in practice, historical significance is necessary to understand the theoretical frameworks, and the research methods implemented within this study. This synthesis aided in understanding the theoretical frameworks describing the relationships between donor motives of providing a monetary donation where the donor did not have a previous relationship with the nonprofit. The next chapter highlights the methods used in this quantitative comparative study to describe the relationship between donor motives and subsequent monetary donation where the donor did not have a previous relationship with a nonprofit Roman Catholic basilica serving visiting tourists in Florida.

Chapter 8: Research Methods

Nonprofits organizations seek to attract new donors when nearly all potential and current donors are decreasing monetary donations to nonprofits in a recessionary United States economy (Arcieri, 2009). Nonprofits must rethink development strategies to attract new donors as well as retain current donors (Durando, 2010). Understanding a donor's motivation to provide a monetary donation to a nonprofit is critical for the organization to achieve necessary philanthropic monetary donations. Data analyses on the motivations of donors who provide a monetary donation to a nonprofit without a previous relationship could assist nonprofit organizations attract new donors. This research could assist the creation and development of new nonprofit organizations. Research conducted to help understand donors' motivations to provide a monetary donation to a nonprofit organization facilitated the exploration, comparison, and understanding of donor motivations to provide a monetary donation to a nonprofit (Burton, 2010; Gaulke, 2010; Lackie, 2010; Mahoney, Gladden, & Funk, 2003; Staurowsky, Parkhouse, & Sachs, 1996; Strode, 2006; Verner, Hecht, & Fansler, 1998).

Research of donor motivations does not provide a singular and reliable motivational theoretical basis. Comprehending a variety of motivational theories is necessary to describe relationships between different donor motivations to provide a monetary donation to a nonprofit when the donor did not have a previous relationship with the nonprofit. Motivational theory based on the Mahoney et al. (2003) and Strode (2006) research is applicable to describe the donor's motivation to provide a monetary donation to a nonprofit. Studies on philanthropic research theories traditionally associated with sales and marketing, integrated with motivation and religion philanthropic theories, provided explanations for a donor to provide a monetary donation to a nonprofit. An investigation of the multiple theoretical works on motivational theory with research in philanthropy, motivation, and religion, could help predict the motivation of a donor to provide a monetary donation to a nonprofit without a previous relationship with the nonprofit.

This quantitative study described the relationships between donor's motivations to provide a monetary donation to a nonprofit without a previous relationship. Comparisons were made of the personal motivations of the target population of donors who provided a monetary donation to a nonprofit Roman Catholic basilica without a previous relationship based on the donor's level of monetary donation. This study incorporated Strode's (2006) survey instrument, with permission, that used multiple motivational theoretical frameworks to test donor motivations providing monetary donations to a nonprofit. The study included an analysis of four motives of achievement, affiliation, philanthropy, and power (independent variables) relative to the monetary donation level (dependent variable). Strode's (2006) validated and reliable survey instrument was designed to minimize respondent error. Strode's (2006) research study focused on the creation of a psychometrically sound survey instrument based on motivational theory that could be used to create donor motivation profiles for nonprofit organizations.

In a setting where donors did not have a previous relationship with a nonprofit, this research incorporated a survey instrument that implemented a quantitative Likert-type scale developed by Strode (2006) to collect data from a target population of 484 donors who provided a monetary donation to a nonprofit basilica in Florida. A test of the sample of 216 participant donors who provided a monetary donation to the basilica revealed if statistical differences exist among the motivations based on McClelland's (1961) theory of needs, in addition to the altruistic helping motive of philanthropy based on Strode's (2006) research. A statistical test of the raw data, collected with participants self-reporting information through the survey instrument, analyzed the motives (independent variables) of achievement, affiliation, and power. The dependent variable is the categorized donor monetary level of donation amount using the participant's self-reported information.

Q1. Is there a statistical difference of the variance among the four motives of achievement, affiliation, philanthropy, and power relative to the level of the monetary donation?

Q2. Is there a statistical correlation between the motivation of achievement on the monetary donation level of a donor who did not have a previous relationship with the nonprofit?

Q3. Is there a statistical correlation between the motivation of affiliation on the monetary donation level of a donor who did not have a previous relationship with the nonprofit?

Q4. Is there a statistical correlation between the motivation of philanthropy on the monetary donation level of a donor who did not have a previous relationship with the nonprofit?

Q5. Is there a statistical correlation between the motivation of power on the monetary donation level of a donor who did not have a previous relationship with the nonprofit?

H1$_0$. There is no statistical difference of the variance among the four motivations of achievement, affiliation, philanthropy, and power relative to the level of the monetary donation.

H1$_a$. There is a statistical difference of the variance among the four motivations of achievement, affiliation, philanthropy, and power relative to the level of the monetary donation.

H2$_0$. There is no statistical correlation between the motivation of achievement relative to the level of the monetary donation.

H2$_a$. There is a statistical correlation between the motivation of achievement relative to the level of the monetary donation.

H3$_0$. There is no statistical correlation between the motivation of affiliation relative to the level of the monetary donation.

H3$_a$. There is a statistical correlation between the motivation of affiliation relative to the level of the monetary donation.

H4$_0$. There is no statistical correlation between the motivation of philanthropy relative to the level of the monetary donation.

H4$_a$. There is a statistical correlation between the motivation of philanthropy relative to the level of the monetary donation.

H5$_0$. There is no statistical correlation between the motivation of power relative to the level of the monetary donation.

H5$_a$. There is a statistical correlation between the motivation of power relative to the level of the monetary donation.

The objective of the respective research questions in this study offered descriptions of the relationships between the donor motivations of achievement, affiliation, philanthropy, and power with donors who did not have a previous relationship with the nonprofit based on the monetary donation level. This study included quantitative data to describe results from the analysis of the different motivations of the sample donors. The four motivations (achievement, affiliation, philanthropy, and power) based on the donors' monetary donation level to a nonprofit basilica, tested theories traditionally associated with sales and marketing along with multiple motivational theories to describe why an individual is compelled to provide a monetary donation to a specific nonprofit without a previous relationship.

The motivations of achievement, affiliation, and power based on McClelland's (1961) theory of needs, along with the altruistic helping motive of philanthropy implemented by Strode (2006), comprised the independent variables in the survey instrument. The categorized monetary donation levels self-reported by the participants represent the dependent variables in this study. Operational definitions of the dependent (level of monetary donation) and independent variables (motivations of achievement, affiliation, philanthropy, and power) appear later in this chapter. The survey instrument incorporated a Likert-type scale to collect interval data using a sample of 216 participants from the target population of 484 donors.

This study used Strode's (2006) survey instrument with permission to collect data to measure motivations of donors providing a monetary donation to a nonprofit without a previous relationship. Strode's survey instrument incorporated McClelland's theory of needs as the theoretical framework, implementing McClelland's needs of achievement, affiliation, and power along with the altruistic helping motive of philanthropy (Strode, 2006). Klebanow and Lowenkopf (1991) explored how monetary donations attributed to an individual donor related to the donor's motivation of power. Individual donors with large financial resources frequently use their monetary resources as a means to achieve power as well as creating a sense of personal achievement (Strode, 2006).

Furnham and Argyle (1998) stated a positive relationship between individual wealth and providing monetary donations to nonprofits. However, Furnham and Argyle (1998) observed that Americans at the top and bottom of personal income levels provide monetary donations at the same frequency (Strode, 2006). Donors providing monetary donations to nonprofits at the highest and lowest monetary donation levels are also similar in frequency (Strode, 2006). However, the motives associated with donors providing a monetary donation may be different (Strode, 2006). This study hypothesized a difference in motives of achievement, affiliation, philanthropy, and power between the five monetary donation levels outlined in the interval Likert-type scales in the survey instrument.

This study implemented quantitative research methodology to describe relationships between donor motivations of donors providing a monetary donation when the donor did not have a previous relationship with the nonprofit by understanding research of philanthropy, human motivation, and religion's role in philanthropy relating to altruistic helping behaviors based on the donor's monetary donation level. The current chapter includes a review of the research methods used in describing relationships of a donor's motivation to provide a monetary donation to a nonprofit without a previous relationship with the donor. This chapter outlines the comparative quantitative research used in this study, which included analysis of the phenomenon of donors providing monetary donations incorporating theoretical frameworks associated with sales and marketing, in addition to multiple motivational theories.

Research Method and Design

This study incorporated quantitative statistical analysis to help describe the relationships between the donor motivations of achievement, affiliation, philanthropy, and power of donors who provided a monetary donation to a nonprofit without a previous relationship. The most suitable quantitative instrument to measure motives and demographics of a sample is a cross-sectional survey (Strode, 2006). According to Zikmund et al. (2009), a cross-sectional survey instrument collects information from a sample at one data collection point from participants. Strode provided written permission to use the survey instrument in this study. The survey instrument was the source of data collection that assisted the descriptions of the attitudes and beliefs of donors providing a monetary donation to a nonprofit (Lind et al., 2011).

This study incorporated the validated and reliable Strode (2006) survey instrument designed to minimize respondent error. Assumptions based on Strode's (2006) validated and reliable survey instrument and research stated the information collected from participants would be accurate and truthful based on quantitative research theory. Strode's (2006) study was focused on the creation of a psychometrically sound survey instrument based on motivational theory that can be used to create donor motivation profiles for nonprofit organizations. The Materials/Instruments section later in this chapter highlights information regarding the reliability and validity of the survey instrument.

A survey completed by the participating donors from the sample of the target population using Strode's (2006) psychometrically valid quantitative survey instrument provided self-reported raw data to measure the individual donor's motivations to provide a monetary donation to the nonprofit basilica. Creswell (2009) stated the post-positive worldview rejects or accepts the hypothesis in quantitative research. The post-positive worldview was the most logical fit to test the hypotheses and answer the question in this study based on literature review, in addition to the Strode survey instrument and research.

A quantitative survey instrument used for data collection facilitated collecting data from participants to answer the research question to describe the individual donor's psychological motivations for providing a monetary donation to a nonprofit. The monetary donations of donors are critical for the nonprofit organization's fundraising staff to achieve the necessary philanthropic organizational funding. The quantitative research framework in this study of motivations of donors providing a monetary donation to a nonprofit where the donor had no previous relationship is germane to statistical data obtained from participants and can directly benefit nonprofits.

This study incorporated an ANOVA that tested the data collected from the participants in the sample of the target population of donors living outside of Florida who provided a monetary donation to the basilica without a previous relationship. Within the study, the ANOVA tests the data of the independent variables (achievement, affiliation, philanthropy, and power) with the dependent variable of the level of donation. The goal of an ANOVA is to determine if statistically significant differences in variances occur between three or more groups (Zikmund et al., 2009).

This study incorporated a single regression analysis. Regression analysis is a test that identifies the statistical correlations between a dependent variable and one or more independent variables (Lind et al., 2011). Graphical representations of the relationship between the variables indicate data used to develop a regression equation (Lind et al., 2011). The statistical data from a single regression analysis results in an equation to predict donor motivations based on the respective donor motivations (independent variable) of achievement, affiliation, philanthropy, and power based on the dependent monetary donation. The single regression analysis used in this study is the simplest form of regression, using a linear bivariate regression to describe a correlation between two variables (Lind et al., 2011). Lind et al. (2011) stated that even though a correlation exists between two variables, a statistical correlation is not causation. A line that graphically represents the data points in a linear correlation may not indicate something definitive about causality (Lind et al., 2011). Zikmund et al. (2009) stated a regression study formulates a hypothesis about the relationship between the variables. This study presented data on the correlations between the respective motivations of achievement, affiliation, philanthropy, and power (independent variable) with the monetary donation level (dependent variable).

Participants

The criteria for participants selected for this study was the target population of new donors who provided a first time monetary donation to the nonprofit Roman Catholic basilica in Florida between January 2010 and June 2010. This study implemented an additional criterion of donors who reside outside of Florida to ensure first time donors who provided a monetary donation to the basilica between January 2010 and June 2010 did not have a previous relationship with the basilica. Information provided by the basilica's rector and director of development identified a target population of 484 donors as first time donors who provided a monetary donation to the basilica between January 2010 and June 2010 while living outside the state of Florida (E. J. McCarthy, personal communication, September 6, 2010). The basilica development staff determined and classified new first time donors based on a monetary donation between January 2010 and June 2010 through maintained, detailed, and accurate records maintained by the basilica development office (E. J. McCarthy, personal communication, June 27, 2009). The participants in the target population of 484 donors resulted in a sample of 216.

Guests visit the basilica for a number of reasons, which can motivate individuals to provide a monetary donation to the nonprofit basilica in Florida. Visitors with various religious faiths and beliefs, come to the basilica to tour the grounds and landscapes, view the unique art and architecture, examine the various museum pieces and collections, shop at the gift shop, attend a basilica choir performance, or attend a Roman Catholic Mass (E. J. McCarthy, personal communication, March 7, 2009). The nonprofit basilica seeks to gain relationships with its donors for the basilica to become a home away from home while guests are visiting the area (E. J. McCarthy, personal communication, June 27, 2009).

Materials/Instruments

The Strode (2006) survey was selected for this study because the instrument was validated to provide data from participant's responses to test data from this study with an analysis of variance (ANOVA) and a single regression analysis. Strode's (2006) study was focused on the creation of a psychometrically sound survey instrument based on motivational theory that can be used to create donor motivation profiles for nonprofit organizations. Strode (2006) validated the survey instrument, used with permission in this study, with a pilot test with a sample of participants of the nonprofit Ohio State University athletic department donors.

Construct validity was tested using item-to-total correlations for the four motivational constructs of achievement, affiliation, philanthropy, and power in the survey instrument validated at Ohio State University (Strode, 2006). The validity and reliability tests conducted by Strode established the survey instrument used in this study accurately measured what the survey intended to measure. Strode (2006) stated it was a necessity to devise a reliable survey instrument to ensure similar participant scores were reflected as comparable for each variable to establish the validity and reliability. Strode's doctoral dissertation committee at Ohio State University approved and validated the reliable survey instrument, which was used in this study to analyze donor's motivations to provide a monetary donation to a nonprofit without a previous relationship.

Strode surveyed a sample of donors providing a monetary donation to a nonprofit university athletic department to complete his doctoral research at Ohio State University. This study also used a sample of nonprofit donors providing a monetary donation to the nonprofit basilica like the nonprofit sample in Strode's study. Strode implemented changes considered critical by the panel of experts, field test, and pilot test at Ohio State University before the final survey distribution to the participants. One of the tests that Strode used was a Cronbach's alpha to determine the internal consistency or average correlation of items used in the survey instrument to measure the reliability (Strode, 2006).

Strode computed four Cronbach's alphas for the motives of affiliation, philanthropy, achievement, and power after using the data from the Strode pilot test at Ohio State University. Strode deemed any alpha value above .70 to be a reliable indicator of Cronbach's alphas for the motives of affiliation, philanthropy, achievement, and power used in the survey instrument. To ensure the construct validity of the survey Strode (2006) used Cronbach's alpha reliabilities that indicated excellent internal reliability with scores over .70. The alpha for the achievement items of the survey instrument was .921, power had .915, philanthropy had .908, and affiliation had a score of .922 (Strode, 2006).

The survey instrument used in this study, used with Strode's permission, incorporated the Strode (2006) validated survey instrument as a tool to describe the motivations of donors providing a monetary donation when participants had no previous relationship with the nonprofit. Within the valid Likert-type scale questionnaire implemented for this study, the motives of affiliation, philanthropy, achievement, and power are the variables used to examine the relationships of the comparative quantitative study through an analysis of variance (ANOVA) using interval data. The study's questionnaire design incorporated a Likert-type scale developed by Strode (2006) to measure the variables (motivations) of affiliation, philanthropy, achievement, and power.

Zikmund et al. (2009) defined a Likert-type scale as being a measure of attitudes designed to allow participants to indicate how strongly they agree or disagree with carefully constructed statements. The statements in questionnaire design scale designed by Strode and used with permission in this study include a range from strongly agree (represented by the numeral 5 in the Likert-type scale), to a neutral position (represented by the numeral 3), and strongly disagree (represented by the numeral 1). A Likert-type scale applied to every question within the validated questionnaire to measure the attitudes of every participant on each respective question using interval data.

In quantitative research, the researcher states an expected occurrence by explaining a relationship between variables by making a research hypothesis. A researcher must choose to either retain or reject the null hypothesis at the beginning of a research study. The rejection of a correct null hypothesis, called a Type I error (symbolized by the Greek letter alpha, α), occurs when a researcher believes there is some sort of relationship even though it does not exist (Lind et al., 2011). A Type II error (symbolized by the Greek letter beta, β) exists when the researcher fails to reject the null hypothesis even though there is a relationship (Lind et al., 2011). Type I and Type II errors are both minimized by setting a significance level (Lind et al., 2011).

Randomly placed throughout the questionnaire, the variable specific survey questions measuring donor motivation assisted with the validity of the responses from participants of this study. The participants were not aware of the consistencies or question patterns of the respective variables (donor motivations) analyzed within the survey. The Strode (2006) survey instrument used in this study implemented a simple and easily understood questionnaire as the questions incorporated a Likert-type scale. Utilizing the Strode (2006) survey instrument, brief and specific questions included in the questionnaire reduced non-response errors. Non-response error can occur based on the subject's lack of interest in the topic surveyed, or unwillingness to be surveyed (Lind et al., 2011). The analysis of the phenomenon of non-response error briefly appears later in this chapter with a detailed analysis contained in the next chapter.

The survey instrument was mailed through the United States Postal Service to the target population in basilica envelopes and stationary to ensure the required sample size to conduct the research. A dated URGENT stamp was placed on the envelope along with the requested response date. Participants would not have received information from the basilica with stamped dated material before this survey mailing. The basilica rector and development staff stated using the basilica stationary with a time sensitive stamp on the envelope would encourage the target population to participate. The basilica had never solicited any information or opinions from its donors in a survey or any other written correspondence. The basilica rector and development staff stated donors would be motivated to respond to share their opinions via a written correspondence and survey instrument based on their knowledge of the population.

Other factors that could have contributed to the reliability and validity of the data included the self -reported information from the participants. The rector of the basilica stated donors who provided a monetary donation to the basilica within the past year would be responsive to generate the required sample to conduct the ANOVA and single regression analysis in this study. The rector based this statement on past response rates from donors responding to basilica development mailings. The rector was confident the participant donors would respond with an acceptable response rate to survey since there was not a request for a monetary donation. The rector of the basilica, who also completed a doctoral dissertation, declared the required response rate based on the power analysis would occur because of the basilica donors' past behavior in addition to the nonprofit basilica being a Roman Catholic house of worship.

The survey instrument did not make allowances for any donor identification to be collected. However, some participant donors could have not responded to the survey because of the expectations of future donations with a survey response. Additional non-response errors could have occurred because some participants could have inflated or deflated their actual donation level reported on the survey. Participants could have felt embarrassed with their actual monetary donation amount and increased the donation level on the survey. Participants who provided larger monetary donation amounts could have reduced the amounts reported in the survey because of perceived requests for increased monetary donations.

Operational Definitions of Variables

Examinations of multiple variables and constructs in this study evaluated donor motives at the nonprofit basilica. Zikmund et al. (2009) defined a variable as anything that can assume different categorical or numerical values, which includes interval scales. To augment validity for this research, the researcher implemented operationally defined variables (motivations). Validity is the ability of a scale or measuring instrument to measure what the scale or instrument intends to measure (Zikmund et al., 2009). An operational definition is a more precise definition designed to illustrate how to calculate a variable within a research study (Lind et al., 2011).

The researcher analyzed four independent variables identified as the donor motivations of power, affiliation, philanthropy, and achievement. This comparative quantitative research provided analysis of the four independent variables through a survey instrument implementing a Likert-type scale, self-reported by the participating donors. The four independent variables determined the relative importance of the respective motives of donors providing a monetary donation to a basilica, the dependent variable used in this study. The survey instrument implemented a 5-point Likert-type scale to collect the participant's motivations (independent variable) to provide a monetary donation to the nonprofit basilica. The dependent variable incorporated in this study was the participant's self-reported monetary donation level.

The questions noted below were not included in the survey instrument in categorical (variable) order. The questions appeared in random listings so the participants could not ascertain the measure of motives in the questionnaire. The participants saw the following questions in the survey instrument to arrange the variables to conduct the ANOVA and single regression analysis. All statements below focus on asking the participants the preface question (I provide to the basilica because).

Achievement.

- I wish the basilica to be the preeminent basilica in the country.

- My donations help in creating the finest shrine facilities and programs.

- I feel pride in the success of the operations at the basilica.

- My donation makes me associated with the success of the basilica.

Power.

- By giving, I can voice my opinion on basilica decisions.

- I can shape the direction of the basilica.

- It allows me to exert influence on decision making at the basilica.

- I receive inside information that is not available to the general public.

Philanthropy.

- Giving to the basilica is the right behavior to engage.

- My gift provides an opportunity to help other visitors.

- My donation makes me experience I am helping others in need.

- I am interested in helping religious charities in need.

  Affiliation.

- By giving, I gain an experience of belongingness at the basilica.

- Associating with the basilica brings me closer to others.

- I enjoy the experience of being a part of a large group of supporters at the Shrine.

- I enjoy an association with other basilica supporters.

- Being a donor allows me to connect with other basilica supporters.

- Being a donor allows me to develop relationships with others.

Achievement. McClelland (1961) defined achievement as an inner need, or drive used to achieve excellence. Staurowsky et al. (1996) explained achievement with the creation of success factors such as loyalty and supporting the nonprofit with both related to the success of the donor. Verner et al. (1998) also related the motive of achievement, and the factors associated with loyalty to the nonprofit and the creation of tangible structures that enable the nonprofit to achieve positive results. Donors may provide a monetary donation to a basilica to seek new ways to grow the reputation, stature, and prominence of the basilica throughout the world. The study measured the achievement variable using a 5-point Likert-type scale. The variable measure attributed a numerical value by assigning numbers from one to five corresponding as 1-Strongly Disagree, 2-Disagree, 3-Neutral, 4-Agree, and 5-Strongly Agree. An ANOVA tested the means for each respective variable.

Affiliation. Affiliation is the positive feeling associated with fitting into a group and a sense of belonging to something more substantive than oneself (Strode, 2006). McClelland (1975) defined affiliation as a motive for harmonious relationships. Other literature refers to the motive in a social vein (Strode, 2006), related to participation in an event with family and friends (Billing et al., 1985), and to the friendships created with the affiliation (Staurowsky et al., 1996). Affiliation represents guests visiting the basilica on family vacations to Florida. Donors can seek affiliation with each other as a part of a unique basilica, which is a cause or a mission larger than himself or herself. A 5-point Likert-type scale measured the affiliation variable in this survey. The variable measure attributed a numerical value by assigning numbers from one to five corresponding as 1-Strongly Disagree, 2-Disagree, 3-Neutral, 4-Agree, and 5-Strongly Agree. An ANOVA tested the means for each respective variable.

Motivation. Maslow (1943) defined motivation as the basis of inspiration and stimulus of desires within human beings to achieve an action based on fulfilling a sequence of needs. Maslow explained motivation as an inner-drive to achieve a goal to satisfy a need. Frankl (1984) believed that man's deepest desire, or motivation, is to search for meaning and purpose in an individual's life. Frankl noted that motivation is a human emotion necessary to achieve a desire or outcome.

Philanthropy. Verner, Hecht, and Fansler (1998) defined philanthropy as an individual making an active effort to promote human welfare, an act of goodwill, or offering assistance to the needy. The concept of philanthropy can be explained in multiple ways, although is summarized by serving and altruistic behaviors (Strode, 2006). Researchers correlated the motive with providing financial sustenance while generating future opportunities for success (Strode, 2006), as well as repaying past benefits received (Mahoney, Gladden, & Funk, 2003). Donors may provide to the basilica for altruistic and philanthropic reasons to assist the poor, assist with future growth projects, or the donors believe providing a monetary donation is an honorable behavior. A 5-point Likert-type scale measured the philanthropy variable on the survey. The variable measure attributed a numerical value by assigning numbers from one to five corresponding as 1-Strongly Disagree, 2-Disagree, 3-Neutral, 4-Agree, and 5-Strongly Agree. An ANOVA tested the means for each respective variable.

Power. Staurowsky, Parkhouse, and Sachs (1996) defined power as opportunities for one person or group of people to exert influence and control over others. Power is associated with influence, access to decision-makers, and inside information (Strode, 2006). Donors who support the basilica may seek to influence decisions and the direction of future basilica growth and projects through the motivation of power. A 5-point Likert-type scale measured the power variable. The variable measure attributed a numerical value by assigning numbers from one to five corresponding as 1-Strongly Disagree, 2-Disagree, 3-Neutral, 4-Agree, and 5-Strongly Agree. An ANOVA tested the means for each respective variable.

Data Collection, Process, and Analysis

This study incorporated Strode's (2006) survey instrument and the tailored design method outlined by Dillman (2000). The Strode research used the tailored design method as well. This study used comprehensive survey research methodology to maximize response rate (Strode, 2006). The tailored design method focused on improving participant response rates by reducing survey errors through the creation of concise questions, appealing mailings, and developing a reward system for participants (Dillman, 2000). The reward system offered by Dillman (2000) was not implemented because of budget constraints with this study. The use of Dillman's (2000) methodology in this research was based on the social exchange theory stated that individuals are motivated by the return of positive behaviors they are expected to receive from others. Strode (2006) noted the social exchange did not need to be for economic gain but could be in altruistic helping behaviors and a feeling of self-satisfaction.

This research began with a mailing sent via the United States Postal Service on September 10, 2010 to a target population of donors (participants) who reside outside the state of Florida and provided a first time monetary donation to the basilica between January 2010 and June 2010. The basilica's rector stated the number of participants fitting the criteria for the target population was 484 (Father E.J. McCarthy, personal communication, June 27, 2009). The written correspondence in the mailing included a cover letter, the questionnaire (survey instrument), instructions, and a self-addressed stamped envelope.

The target population of first time donors who provided a monetary donation to the basilica between January 2010 and June 2010 had reasonable expectations to receive information from the basilica. The basilica envelopes, affixed with an October 25, 2010 URGENT stamp on the front, helped ensure the necessary response rate for the sample based on the power analysis. The October 25, 2010 date also allowed for an additional postcard mailing if the response rate from the initial mailing was not 35% after three weeks. Based on the rector's knowledge of basilica development efforts, and this study implementing the Dallman (2000) tailored design method, the rector stated an acceptable response rate would be achieved in this study. Participants completed and returned a survey with an enclosed stamped envelope with the basilica's mailing address in addition to a sticker labeled Olszewski-NCU as the return address.

Returned unopened surveys were collected every week from the time of the initial mailing on September 10, 2010 to October 25, 2010. The researcher opened and analyzed the surveys to ensure completeness and usability. Raw data was inputted utilizing a personal computer and the Statistical Package for the Social Sciences (SPSS) 17.0 from the 216 usable surveys completed with the directions provided to the participants. A colleague of the researcher with a graduate degree checked the data entry procedures by the primary researcher to ensure accuracy of the data entry. To determine the null hypothesis and the alternative hypothesis in this study, an analysis of variance tested the independent variables of achievement, affiliation, philanthropy, and power with the dependent variable of the monetary donation level utilizing Statistical Package for the Social Sciences (SPSS) 17.0. To ensure reliability and validity of the research, participants selected for the study were donors who reside outside Florida and provided a first time monetary donation to the basilica between January 2010 and June 2010. The participants represented the entire target population of 484 basilica donors fitting the criteria that generated a sample of 216 participants.

High (2000) stated that power analysis is a statistical test of the probability the test will reject the null hypothesis when the null hypothesis is false (not make a Type II error). According to High, as the power increases, the chances of a Type II error occurring decreases whereas the probability of a Type II error occurring is referred to as the false negative rate (β). Known as the sensitivity, power is equal to $1 - \beta$ (High, 2000). A power analysis is appropriate when the concern is with the correct rejection, or not, of a null hypothesis (High, 2000). Power analysis applies to an ANOVA to assess the probability of successfully rejecting the null hypothesis based on the ANOVA design, effect size of the population, sample size, and alpha level.

Using the G*Power computer program (Erdfelder, Faul, & Buchner, 1996) the required sample size for the study was determined. The power analysis was based on an alpha level of .05, two-tailed tests, and desired power of .80. Based on the G*Power, the sample size of 45 would have been required to have a reasonable chance of rejecting the null hypothesis when the alternative hypothesis was true based on a one-way ANOVA with four groups (Cohen, 1992). With a total target population of 484 utilized in this study, a power analysis helped establish the minimum number of an acceptable sample size of 45 required to identify an effect of a specific size with an ANOVA including four groups (Cohen, 1992). Within a power analysis, the sample size determines the amount of sampling error inherent in a test result. Increasing sample size is often the easiest way to boost the statistical power of a test. For this study, 216 out of the 484 donors fitting the criteria of the target population responded, which resulted in a sample size of 216.

Selecting a target population of participants to participate in the survey was critical to the quantitative research (Zikmund et al., 2009). To ensure the sample from a target population could accurately represent and generalize a population, applicable research strata designs were incorporated within the study. Using Strode's (2006) validated survey instrument ensured the items generated and selected in the instrument measured what the survey signifies to measure based on theory. Careful wording of each question ensured the goal of minimizing confusion for the participants (Strode, 2006). An analysis of variance (ANOVA) and a single regression analysis were used to test the hypotheses with the collected participant survey data in this study.

Within the study, the ANOVA tests the data of the independent variables (achievement, affiliation, philanthropy, and power) with the dependent variable of the level of donation. The goal of an ANOVA is to determine if statistically significant differences in variances occur between three or more groups (Zikmund et al., 2009). A Bonferroni adjustment could have been used in the ANOVA to ensure the experiment error rate be relegated to a specified level during the ANOVA analysis, usually α equals .05 (Estes, 1991). However, this study implemented a Levene's test to address the unequal balance in the groups of the monetary donation levels.

According to Zikmund et al. (2009), the Levene's test assesses the null hypothesis the variances of the group are the same as the probability that a sample in the test has a significantly different variance. Implementing a Levene's test where the results provide a statistical significance greater than .05, the variances are too large to apply the ANOVA test (Zikmund et al., 2009). An ANOVA test assumes the variances of the groups are equal, whereas a Homogeneity of Variances test (Levene's) proves the assumption that variances were equal in the groups to accurately implement the ANOVA (Zikmund et al., 2009). The ANOVA test in the study assessed the independent variables (achievement, affiliation, philanthropy, and power) with the dependent variable of the level of donation. The variances in the study were equal when observing the inferential statistic results from the Homogeneity of Variances (Levene's) test (Zikmund et al., 2009). The ANOVA is valid when the results of the Levene's test are not statistically significant (Zikmund et al., 2009).

Zikmund et al. (2009) stated that a single regression analysis is a statistical test for analyzing variables of the relationship between a dependent variable and one or more independent variables. A single regression analysis is a test that outlines the value of the dependent variable when any one of the independent variables is varied (Zikmund et al., 2009). Research studies include a single regression analysis to understand which of the independent variables are related to the dependent variable while exploring relationships (Lind et al., 2011).

Methodological Assumptions, Limitations, and Delimitations

This quantitative research methodology used in the study based on the power analysis assumed the target population of 484 basilica donors meeting the criteria set forth in this study would generate a sample of 214 provided by the power analysis. Assumptions maintained in this study suggested that participants would provide truthful responses with a response rate that would provide validation of the sample to conduct this study as well as the ANOVA and single regression analysis. Limitations included participants self-reporting data within the comparative quantitative study. Participants who completed the questionnaire could have misinterpreted the questions in the survey. Accuracy of the participant's mailing addresses provided by the basilica is essential assumptions that could limit this study. Because the donors provided a monetary donation to the basilica within the past calendar year, the address provided by the basilica for the research was assumed accurate, thus increasing the response rate.

Limitations of the study included the basilica wanting to protect the identity of its donors. The basilica did not permit gender identification and other demographic information within the study's survey instrument. Having gender and other demographic information as variables for future research would provide deeper understanding of a potential donor profile to provide a monetary donation to a nonprofit organization. The data collected to conduct an ANOVA and a single regression analysis in this study are from one unique sample from one specific nonprofit. This study surveyed a target population from one nonprofit institution. Utilizing one nonprofit organization made it difficult to generalize the results to dissimilar nonprofit entities. The basilica was selected as the nonprofit in this study because the basilica met the characteristics of first time donors having no previous relationship with a nonprofit.

Discussed in a previous section of the chapter, steps ensured both the reliability and validity for the research design and methods used to survey the participants to test the hypotheses and answer the research question. Participants self-reporting data was a legitimate limitation of the comparative quantitative study. Participants who completed the questionnaire could have misinterpreted the questions, and the validity of the donor's mailing address provided by the basilica rector and development staff. The basilica's development staff provided the addresses directly from their donor lists as well as the most accurate information of the donors fitting the research criteria. The research did not identify any returned envelopes because of inaccurate addresses.

Implementation of sound research strategies ensure the participants could complete the questionnaire to provide valid data. To ensure internal validity, many measures needed to be defined and evaluated. To understand the variables in both definition and theory, Zikmund et al. (2009) stated a researcher could only observe the impact the independent variable has on the dependent variable, as no manipulation of either variable ensures adherence of construct validity standards. Construct validity is the ability of a measure to confirm a network of related hypotheses generated from a theory based on the concepts (Zikmund et al., 2009). The four independent variables were attributed numerical values from one to five corresponding as 1-Strongly Disagree, 2-Disagree, 3-Neutral, 4-Agree, and 5-Strongly Agree. An ANOVA tested the means for each respective independent variable under the quantitative theoretical framework.

Zikmund et al. (2009) stated an assumption of an ANOVA is groups follow the normal curve, an assumption made in most significance tests. An ANOVA applies two or more groups at once as many distributions do not follow the normal curve, thus an ANOVA may provide incorrect results (Zikmund et al., 2009). A Levene's Test (Homogeneity of Variance) ensures the validity of an ANOVA when groups are not equal. Levene's test tests the null hypothesis of the variances of the group are the same (Zikmund et al., 2009). The output probability of the Levene's test is the probability that at least one of the samples in the test has a significantly different variance (Zikmund et al., 2009).

The survey participants could have caused threats to the internal validity during this experiment, such as changing views or experiences of the question (Creswell, 2009). Creswell (2009) stated that construct validity is an issue when researchers use inadequate definitions and measures of variables. Incorporating a Likert-type scale, the data gathered from the survey

instrument tests the hypotheses by implementing an analysis of variance (ANOVA) and a single

regression analysis. Within the study, the ANOVA tested the mean effects of the independent

variables (achievement, affiliation, philanthropy, and power) with the dependent variable based

on the level of donation with a valid survey instrument consisting of carefully worded questions.

A delimitation of the study was the data used to conduct an ANOVA and single

regression analysis was collected from one unique sample from a target population from one

specific nonprofit. The nonprofit basilica fit the criteria for donors having no previous

relationship with the nonprofit as first time donors. This study incorporated one nonprofit to

generalize the results to other nonprofits organizations for donors to provide a monetary

donation. The basilica does not have any church members and does not benefit from any

monetary support from the local Catholic diocese, as the financial support must come from

guests visiting the basilica (Father E.J. McCarthy, personal communication, March 7, 2009).

The financial sustenance and maintenance of the national basilica relies almost exclusively on

the philanthropic generosity of guest and tourists who are potential donors (E. J. McCarthy,

personal communication, March 7, 2009). Selecting the basilica donors at the nonprofit to

survey narrowed the scope of the study.

Ethical Assurances

The design of this study complied with the standards of conducting research with human

participants set forth by Northcentral University. The researcher did not collect personal

identification because of the basilica not wanting any identifiable demographic information on

the surveys. The cover letter informed the participants that participation was voluntary.

Participants in the target population could not participate by simply electing not to complete the survey. Assurances within the cover letter that accompanied the survey informed participants that no means were available to track identification or participation in the study. All participants who completed the survey would be anonymous.

The participants received a set of instructions with the cover letter in addition to the quantitative survey instrument to communicate instructions for their participation in this research study. The instructions included the directions of this research and the required information for addressing informed consent guidelines developed by Northcentral University's Internal Review Board (IRB). This study received approval from Northcentral University's IRB prior to any data collection. The surveys collected from the participants are stored in a locked file cabinet in the researcher's office to ensure the security of the data.

Summary

This study incorporated research literature from philanthropy, human motivation, and religion's role in philanthropy relating to altruistic helping behaviors. Quantitative research methodology guided this study to describe relationships among donor motivations to provide a monetary donation to a nonprofit when the donor had no previous relationship with the nonprofit. This chapter included a summary of the quantitative research methods implemented in this study to collect, process, and analyze data. This comparative quantitative research incorporated examinations of theoretical frameworks associated with sales and marketing, in addition to multiple motivational theories to answer the research question outlined in this study.

The research question aided the descriptions of the relationships between motivations of donors to provide a monetary donation to a nonprofit when the donor did not have a previous relationship with the nonprofit. An ANOVA test provided data to assist the descriptions of the differences between the motivations of donors based on the monetary donation level. The four motivations (achievement, affiliation, philanthropy, and power) based on the donors' monetary donation level to a nonprofit basilica in Florida were analyzed. The ANOVA was validated by the Levene's test. This research incorporated theories associated with sales and marketing along with multiple motivational theories in evaluating why a donor provided a monetary donation to a nonprofit. The research question established if relationships could be described between the motivations of achievement, affiliation, philanthropy, and power of donors providing a monetary donation when the individual donor did not have any previous relationship with the nonprofit based on the donation level. The Null Hypothesis stated there is no difference among the four motives of achievement, affiliation, philanthropy, and power relative to the donation level. Whereas the Alternative Hypothesis stated there is a difference among the four motives of achievement, affiliation, philanthropy, and power relative to the donation level. The next chapter will present the research findings from the quantitative comparative study.

CHAPTER 10: FINDINGS

This quantitative study described the relationships between motivations of donors based on the monetary donation level of donors who provided a monetary donation to a nonprofit without having a previous relationship with the nonprofit. Statistical tests were conducted of the personal motivations of the target population of first time donors who provided a monetary donation to a nonprofit Roman Catholic basilica in Florida without a previous relationship. This study incorporated, with permission, Strode's (2006) survey instrument that incorporated multiple motivational theoretical frameworks to test donor motivations providing monetary donations to a nonprofit. This study included an analysis of four donor motivations of achievement, affiliation, philanthropy, and power (independent variables) relative to the donor's monetary donation level (dependent variable). This research sought to answer a question if there was a statistical difference of the variance among the motivations of achievement, affiliation, philanthropy, and power based on the monetary donation level of a donor who did not have a previous relationship with a nonprofit. Additionally, an analysis tested the questions if there was a statistical correlation between the respective motivations of achievement, affiliation, philanthropy, and power on the monetary donation level of a donor who did not have a previous relationship with the nonprofit.

The Strode (2006) survey was selected for this study because the instrument was validated to provide data from participant's responses to test data from this study with an analysis of variance (ANOVA) and a single regression analysis. Strode's (2006) validated and reliable survey instrument was designed by Strode to minimize respondent error which held that correct assumptions of data from the survey was accurate and truthful based on quantitative research theory. Strode's (2006) psychometrically valid quantitative survey instrument was sent to the target population of 484 donors who reside outside of Florida and provided a monetary donation to a nonprofit basilica resulting in a sample of 216 participants. The nonprofit basilica in this study serves tourists and guests in a city in Florida as the target population only included first time donors who did not have a previous relationship with the nonprofit basilica.

This chapter outlines the results from this quantitative comparative study, which describes the relationship between motivations of donors providing a monetary donation to a nonprofit without a previous relationship. The design of this research study compared personal motivations of individual donors who provided a monetary donation to a nonprofit Roman Catholic basilica in Florida, which the donors had no previous relationship. This chapter contains data analysis that outlined the findings from this study that described relationships between donor motivations (independent variables) to provide a monetary donation to nonprofit when the individual donor did not have any previous relationship with the nonprofit based on the monetary donation level (dependent variable).

This study's research questions as well as the respective null and alternative hypotheses served as the organizational outline for this chapter. The data analysis provided the results to answer Research Question 1 if there was a statistical difference of the variance among the motivations of achievement, affiliation, philanthropy, and power based on the monetary donation level of a donor who did not have a previous relationship with the nonprofit. The data analysis provided the results to answer Research Questions 2-5 if there was a statistical correlation between the respective motivations of achievement, affiliation, philanthropy, and power on the monetary donation level of a donor who did not have a previous relationship with the nonprofit. The results of this study are presented in this section organized with the following research questions and hypotheses.

Q1. Is there a statistical difference of the variance among the four motives of achievement, affiliation, philanthropy, and power relative to the level of the monetary donation?

Q2. Is there a statistical correlation between the motivation of achievement on the monetary donation level of a donor who did not have a previous relationship with the nonprofit?

Q3. Is there a statistical correlation between the motivation of affiliation on the monetary donation level of a donor who did not have a previous relationship with the nonprofit?

Q4. Is there a statistical correlation between the motivation of philanthropy on the monetary donation level of a donor who did not have a previous relationship with the nonprofit?

Q5. Is there a statistical correlation between the motivation of power on the monetary donation level of a donor who did not have a previous relationship with the nonprofit?

$\mathbf{H1_0}$. There is no statistical difference of the variance among the four motivations of achievement, affiliation, philanthropy, and power relative to the level of the monetary donation.

$\mathbf{H1_a}$. There is a statistical difference of the variance among the four motivations of achievement, affiliation, philanthropy, and power relative to the level of the monetary donation.

$\mathbf{H2_0}$. There is no statistical correlation between the motivation of achievement relative to the level of the monetary donation.

$\mathbf{H2_a}$. There is a statistical correlation between the motivation of achievement relative to the level of the monetary donation.

H3$_0$. There is no statistical correlation between the motivation of affiliation relative to the level of the monetary donation.

H3$_a$. There is a statistical correlation between the motivation of affiliation relative to the level of the monetary donation.

H4$_0$. There is no statistical correlation between the motivation of philanthropy relative to the level of the monetary donation.

H4$_a$. There is a statistical correlation between the motivation of philanthropy relative to the level of the monetary donation.

H5$_0$. There is no statistical correlation between the motivation of power relative to the level of the monetary donation.

H5$_a$. There is a statistical correlation between the motivation of power relative to the level of the monetary donation.

Results

The target population 484 participants included first time donors who reside outside of Florida and provided a monetary donation to the nonprofit basilica between January and June of 2010. The members of the target population received the survey in the United States mail. The 484 surveys sent to target population resulted in 220 returned surveys that resulted in a 45.5% response rate from the target population. This study included a sample of 216 participants, as four surveys returned were incomplete and unusable because of respondent error.

Descriptive statistics. The results in Table 2 list the monetary donation level frequencies reported by the participants from the sample from this study. The results generated from the data analysis of the monetary donation frequencies demonstrated as the monetary donation level increased, the number of participants who provided at that monetary donation level decreased.

The pattern did not deviate until the highest monetary donation level because of the unlimited monetary donation option offered to participants as a choice within the Likert-type scale. The frequency statistics in Table 3 highlight the results based on the donor's motivations with the categorical monetary donation levels.

Table 2

Donation Frequencies

Donors	$1-99	$100-199	$200-299	$300-399	$400 >	Totals
Frequency	110	62	20	10	14	216
Percent	50.9	28.7	9.3	4.6	6.5	100
Cumulative	50.9	79.6	88.9	93.5	100	

Table 3

Average Frequency Statistics

	Donation	Achievement	Affiliation	Philanthropy	Power
Mean	1.87	3.7	3.2	4.0	2.9
Median	1.00	3.8	3.2	4.0	3.0
Mode	1	3.8	3.0	4.0	3.0
Std. Deviation	1.166	.833	.877	.617	.944
Variance	1.360	.695	.770	.382	.892

The frequency statistics outlined that 216 participants responded with a 1.87 mean score for monetary donation levels as most donors in this study provided a monetary donation less than $99. The lowest observed total group mean ratings were for power (M=2.8, SD=.94) and affiliation (M=3.2, SD=.88) motivation factors. The highest observed total group mean ratings were for philanthropy (M=4.0, SD=.62) and achievement (M=3.7, SD=.83) motivation factors. The lowest observed total group median and mode ratings were for power (median=3.0, mode=3.0) and affiliation (median =3.2, mode=3.0) motivation factors. The highest median and mode ratings were for philanthropy (median =4.0, mode=4.0) and achievement (median=3.8, mode=3.8) motivation factors. The descriptive statistics from the 216 participants include the means and standard deviations with the respective monetary donation levels and totals are included in Tables 4-8.

Table 4

Descriptive Statistics of Achievement with Means and Standard Deviations

Motivation	Donation	N	Mean	Std. Deviation	Std. Error
Achievement	$1-99	110	3.5	.839	.080
	$100-199	62	3.9	.761	.096
	$200-299	20	4.0	.825	.184
	$300-399	10	4.0	.677	.214
	$400 >	14	4.0	.854	.228
Totals		216	3.7	.833	.056

Table 5

Descriptive Statistics of Affiliation with Means and Standard Deviations

Motivation	Donation	N	Mean	Std. Deviation	Std. Error
Affiliation	$1-99	110	3.1	.827	.078
	$100-199	62	3.4	.895	.113
	$200-299	20	3.3	1.068	.238
	$300-399	10	3.2	.981	.310
	$400 >	14	3.4	.820	.219
Totals		216	3.2	.877	.059

Table 6

Descriptive Statistics of Philanthropy with Means and Standard Deviations

Motivation	Donation	N	Mean	Std. Deviation	Std. Error
Philanthropy	$1-99	110	3.9	.646	.061
	$100-199	62	4.2	.505	.064
	$200-299	20	4.1	.635	.142
	$300-399	10	4.0	.660	.209
	$400 >	14	4.2	.616	.164
Totals		216	4.0	.617	.042

Table 7

Descriptive Statistics of Power with Means and Standard Deviations

Motivation	Donation	N	Mean	Std. Deviation	Std. Error
Power	$1-99	110	2.7	.838	.079
	$100-199	62	3.1	.997	.126
	$200-299	20	2.8	1.163	.260
	$300-399	10	2.9	1.001	.316
	$400 >	14	2.9	1.077	.287
Totals		216	2.8	.944	.064

Table 8

Descriptive Statistics Motivation Totals with Means and Standard Deviations

Motivation	N	Mean	Std. Deviation	Std. Error
Achievement	216	3.7	.833	.056
Affiliation	216	3.2	.877	.059
Philanthropy	216	4.0	.617	.042
Power	216	2.8	.944	.064

The results from the data analysis based on the mean score represent the motivations of donors to provide a monetary donation to the basilica. The highest observed total group mean ratings were for philanthropy (M=4.0, SD=.62) and achievement (M=3.7, SD=.83) motivation factors. The lowest observed total group mean ratings were for power (M=2.8, SD=.94) and affiliation (M=3.2, SD=.88) motivation factors.

Within each monetary donation level category, the philanthropy donor motivation earned the highest mean score. The power donor motivation earned the lowest mean score in each monetary donation level category. The donor motivation of achievement mean score increased as the participants provided monetary donations at higher monetary donation levels. The donor motivation of philanthropy mean score generally decreased as donors provided a monetary donation at a higher monetary donation level. The results observing the standard deviation in this study followed the same pattern as the mean score in the donor motivations of philanthropy and power. The standard deviation represented the variation from the mean, statistically described as the square root of the variance, which provided evidence to examine the research question of differences among the four variables of achievement, affiliation, philanthropy, and power.

Research Question 1 was framed to explore if there was a statistical difference of the variance among the four motives of achievement, affiliation, philanthropy, and power relative to the level of the monetary donation. The participants identified their monetary donation level utilizing a Likert-type scale incorporated in the survey instrument. Two studies (Mahony et al., 2003; Strode, 2006) have empirically tested the relationship of the motivations of donors providing a monetary donation to a nonprofit as conducted in this study. A one-way ANOVA was conducted to test Hypothesis 1 and the differences of the variance among the four motives of achievement, affiliation, philanthropy, and power based on Strode (2006) and McClelland's (1963) needs theory.

Research question 1. The observations of the inferential statistic results from the ANOVA of the variances in the groups are assumed equal. The significant results from the ANOVA test for the motivations of donors providing a monetary donation to a nonprofit when the donor did not have a previous relationship were achievement F (3, 212) = 4.07, p = .003 and philanthropy F (3, 212) = 2.97, p = .020. The data analysis from the one-way ANOVA with four groups provided results that donor motivations of achievement and philanthropy were significant to the donor's monetary donation level. The donors were divided into four group based on the participants' self-selected motivations by completing the survey. The level of donation was treated as a continuous, interval-level variable to conduct the one-way ANOVA.

Hypothesis 1. The null hypothesis was structured to outline there is no statistical difference among the four motivations of achievement, affiliation, philanthropy, and power relative to the level of the monetary donation. The alternative hypothesis was structured there is a statistical difference among variance of the four motivations of achievement, affiliation, philanthropy, and power relative to the level of the monetary donation. In each monetary donation level category, philanthropy earned the lowest deviation whereas the power donor motivation had the largest deviation in four of five monetary donation level categories. To validate the one-way ANOVA with four groups used in this study, a Homogeneity of Variances test (Levene's) assessed the assumption that variances in the groups were equal with the Levene's test results presented in Table 9. The ANOVA results listed in Table 10 illustrate the relationships between different motives.

Table 9

Test of Homogeneity of Variances

Variables	Levene Statistic	p
Achievement	.262	.902
Affiliation	.554	.696
Philanthropy	.839	.502
Power	1.360	.249

Table 10

ANOVA

Source	Motivations	df	F	p
Donors	Achievement	3	4.068	.003
	Affiliation	3	.947	.438
	Philanthropy	3	2.971	.020
	Power	3	1.261	.286

Table 11

Reliability Statistics Cronbach's Alphas

Cronbach's Alphas	Number of Questions
.916	18

The non-significant results were confirmed through the Levene's Test, which validated the ANOVA test that assumed the variances of the groups are equal. The ANOVA test assessed the independent variables (achievement, affiliation, philanthropy, and power) with the dependent variable of the monetary donation level. The Homogeneity of Variances (Levene's) test provided non-significant results that validated the ANOVA used to test the data in this study.

The data analysis provided specific findings that motivations influenced the level of donors providing a monetary donation to a nonprofit. The lowest observed standard deviations in the monetary donation levels were for power (SD=.94) and affiliation (SD=.88) motivation factors. The highest standard deviations in the monetary donation levels were for philanthropy (SD=.62) and achievement (SD=.83) motivation factors. The results did not suggest that different motives of achievement, affiliation, philanthropy, and power influenced different monetary donation levels provided by donors. The result from Hypothesis 1 outlined there was no significance of the motivations of achievement, affiliation, philanthropy, and power relative to the monetary donation levels.

To determine the internal consistency of the survey questions measuring the motives of affiliation, philanthropy, achievement, and power, Strode (2006) computed four Cronbach's alphas using data from that pilot study prior to using the survey instrument. The reliability statistic Cronbach's alpha implemented in this study tested the internal reliability of the questions used with Strode's permission after conducting an ANOVA test. After conducting the ANOVA test, a Cronbach's alpha test with 18 items provided a score of .92 representing the internal reliability of the questions used in this study. Based on Cronbach's alpha, the survey indicated a high level of internal consistency (18 items; $\alpha = .92$).

Regression analysis. To determine which motivations of achievement, affiliation, philanthropy, and power are correlated with the monetary donation level, this study incorporated a single regression analysis. The single regression analysis was conducted to test Hypotheses 2-5, which postulated correlations between the respective motivations of achievement, affiliation, philanthropy, and power of basilica donors based on the monetary donation level. The dependent variable for the single regression analysis was the monetary donation level. Using the dependent variable of the monetary donation level, four single regressions respectively tested the respective motivations of achievement, affiliation, philanthropy, and power.

The data from the single regression analysis from this study indicated the motivations of achievement and philanthropy did produce significant results whereas affiliation and power did not produce significant results. The results from the single regression analyses are in Tables 12-15. Figures 5 and 6 graphically outline a positive linear relationships of the significant motivations of achievement and philanthropy from data obtained from the single regression

analysis.

Research question 2. The research question was framed to explore if there is a statistical

correlation between the motivation of achievement relative to the monetary donation level of a

donor who did not have a previous relationship with the nonprofit. Table 12 lists the results from

the single regression analysis for the achievement variable. The results of the regression

provided a negligible R^2 score but did result in a strong linear relationship with the achievement

motivation provided later in this chapter in Figure 5.

Table 12

Summary of Single Regression Analysis for the Achievement Variable

Motivation		B	β
Achievement		.32	.23
R^2	.05		
F	*11.4*		

Hypothesis 2. The null hypothesis was structured to outline there is no statistical

correlation between the motivation of achievement relative to the level of the monetary donation.

The alternative hypothesis was structured there is a statistical correlation between the motivation

of achievement relative to the level of the monetary donation. The achievement motivation

resulted in a strong linear relationship from the single regression analysis presented in Figure 5.

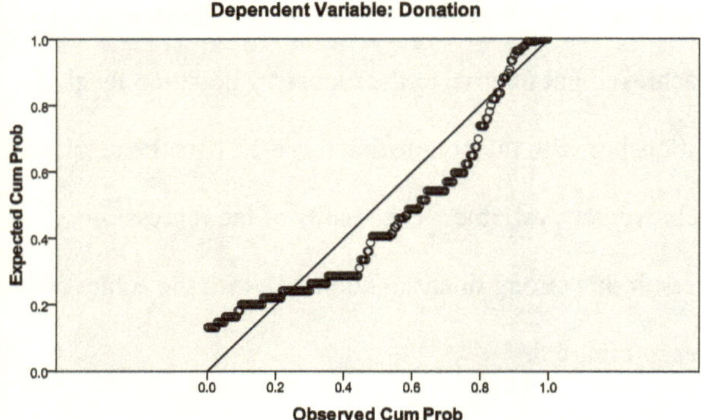

Figure 5. Normal P-P Plot of Regression Standardized Residual for Achievement Motivation.

Research question 3. The research question was framed to explore if there is a statistical correlation between the motivation of affiliation relative to the monetary donation level of a donor who did not have a previous relationship with the nonprofit. Table 13 lists the results from the single regression analysis for the affiliation variable. The results of the regression provided a negligible R^2 score and did not result in a strong linear relationship with the affiliation motivation.

Table 13

Summary of Single Regression Analysis for the Affiliation Variable

Motivation		B	β
Affiliation		.19	.09
R^2	.01		
F	1.7		

Research question 4. The research question was framed to explore if there is a statistical correlation between the motivation of philanthropy relative to the monetary donation level of a donor who did not have a previous relationship with the nonprofit. Table 14 lists the results from the single regression analysis for the philanthropy variable. The results of the regression provided a negligible R^2 score but did result in a strong linear relationship with the philanthropy motivation provided later in this section in Figure 6.

Table 14

Summary of Single Regression Analysis for the Philanthropy Variable

Motivation	B	β
Philanthropy	.31	.16
R^2 .03		
F 5.7		

Hypothesis 4. The null hypothesis was structured to outline there is no statistical correlation between the motivation of philanthropy relative to the level of the monetary donation. The alternative hypothesis was structured there is a statistical correlation between the motivation of philanthropy relative to the level of the monetary donation. The philanthropy motivation resulted in a strong linear relationship from the single regression analysis presented in Figure 6.

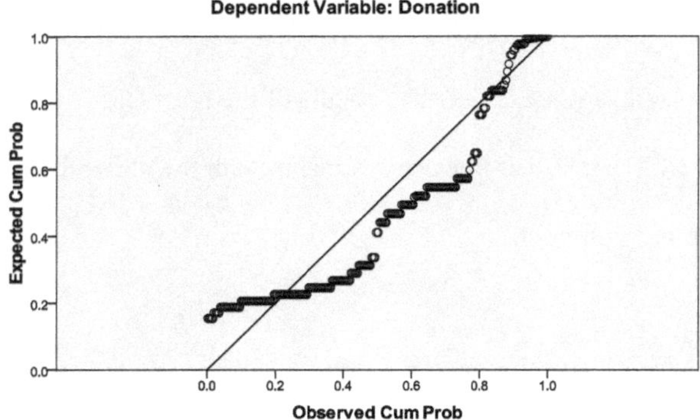

Figure 6. Normal P-P Plot of Regression Standardized Residual for Philanthropy Motivation.

The results from the single regression analysis denoted a positive linear relationship between the statistical significant motivations of achievement and philanthropy with the dependent variable of the monetary donation. The significant data results from the single regression analysis indicated the motivations of achievement $B = -.23$, $t(3.38) = .00$, $p < .05$ and philanthropy $B = -.16$, $t(2.39) = .02$, $p < .05$ had a statistical correlation and a positive linear relationship with the level of giving. The coefficient for achievement is .315, which indicated for every unit increase in the achievement motivation, a .32 unit increase in the monetary donation level is predicted with the constant variables.

Standardizing the variables before conducting the single regression analysis allows for comparisons of the effects of the magnitude of the coefficients as all of the variables are on the same scale. The coefficient for the achievement motivation (.32) is significant because the p-value is .00, smaller than .05. The coefficient for philanthropy is .305, which indicates every unit increase in the philanthropy motivation, a .31 unit increase in the monetary donation level is predicted with the variables constant. The coefficient for philanthropy (.31) is significant because the p-value is .02, smaller than .05.

Research question 5. The research question was framed to explore if there is a statistical correlation between the motivation of power on the monetary donation level of a donor who did not have a previous relationship with the nonprofit. Table 15 lists the results from the single regression analysis for the power variable. The results of the regression provided a negligible R^2 score and did not result in a strong linear relationship with the power motivation.

Table 15

Summary of Single Regression Analysis for the Power Variable

Motivation		B	β
Power		.07	.06
R^2	.003		
F	*.69*		

Evaluation of Findings

Previous research has implied that motivations are related to a nonprofit donor's monetary donation levels, however, these previous studies have not tested this relationship. Previous research by Mahony et al. (2003) and Strode (2006) empirically tested this relationship between donor motivations and monetary donation levels. Both Mahony et al. (2003) and Strode (2006) discovered no significant correlations in monetary donation level based on different motives achievement, affiliation, philanthropy, and power.

Research question 1. This research question was framed to explore if there was a statistical difference of the variance among the four motives of achievement, affiliation, philanthropy, and power relative to the level of the monetary donation. The results of this comparative quantitative research are the donor motivations of achievement, affiliation, philanthropy, and power of donor who provide a monetary donation to a nonprofit when the individual donor had no previous relationship the nonprofit. Academic researchers have examined individual motivations when providing monetary donations to various nonprofits including churches and single congregations. Psychological and sociological researchers have also investigated motivation of donors, presenting reasons donor provide a monetary donation to a nonprofit.

Historically, nonprofit organizations have researched business frameworks that observed motivations of donors providing a monetary philanthropic donation. This quantitative comparative study was significant because it combined distinct philanthropy, motivation, and business fields and synthesized the research into an underrepresented study within the business development and philanthropic research fields. This research added new knowledge to multiple theoretical frameworks based on the analysis of donor motivations to provide a monetary donation to a nonprofit Roman Catholic basilica where the donors did not have a previous relationship.

Mahony et al. (2003) and Strode (2006) empirically tested the relationship of the motivations of donors providing a monetary donation to a nonprofit. This quantitative study is significant as the findings added new knowledge to the business development field by analyzing the donor motivations to a nonprofit organization where the donors did not have a previous relationship with the nonprofit organization. Mahony et al. (2003) and Strode (2006) revealed significant differences in motivations of donors to provide a monetary donation to a nonprofit. Their research suggested that different motives were not predictive of donors providing a nonprofit with different monetary donation levels. This research outlined evidence to support both the Mahony et al. and Strode research that some motivations influence donors to provide a monetary donation to a nonprofit.

The statistical significance of achievement and philanthropy from this study as psychological motivations describe the relationships of donor motivation of donors providing a monetary donation to a nonprofit when the donor had no previous relationship with the nonprofit provide further philanthropic and donor insights. As evident with Locke (2002) and Frankl (1984), both researchers stated that living a life with meaning is a basic human motivation achieved through suffering, self-sacrifice, and taking a stand toward conditions through philanthropic actions. Many Christian faiths, including Roman Catholicism, believe in self-sacrifice in addition to taking a position to serve those in need. The findings from this research provides support with Locke (2002) and Frankl (1984) that donors of the nonprofit Roman Catholic basilica provided a monetary donation for philanthropic motivations by making a self-sacrifice as well serving those in need.

When the participants visited the basilica while on vacation, they could have an increased motivation to provide a specific monetary donation because of their personal travel, hoping to improve conditions for future guests at a house of worship serving other individuals in similar conditions to their own. However, Locke's (2002) research presented that motivation is more than merely alleviating suffering of others, as service in the church provided more meaning in life than only weekly church attendance. Participants in the study experienced the basilica while on vacation or traveling, and by providing a monetary donation to a nonprofit where they had no previous relationship, the participants may have fulfilled their need to serve the church and by providing financial support to those in need, which demonstrated both motivations of achievement and philanthropy.

Hypothesis 1. The null hypothesis was structured to outline there is no statistical difference among the four motivations of achievement, affiliation, philanthropy, and power relative to the level of the monetary donation. The alternative hypothesis was structured to outline there is a statistical difference of the variance among the four motivations of achievement, affiliation, philanthropy, and power relative to the level of the monetary donation. The basis for the rejection of the null Hypothesis 1 is the evidence from the data analysis because there was a difference among the four motives of achievement, affiliation, philanthropy, and power relative to the monetary donation level.

Analysis of the data offered evidence for the acceptance of the alternative hypothesis because there was a difference among the four motives of achievement, affiliation, philanthropy, and power based on the monetary donation level. The participant's responses represented in the mean scores illustrated donor's highest motivation to provide a monetary donation to the nonprofit basilica was achievement, followed by philanthropy, affiliation, and power. Mahony et al. (2003) and Strode (2006) also revealed significant differences in motivations of donors to provide a monetary donation to a nonprofit. The alternative hypothesis accepted in this research study maintained there was a statistical difference in the independent variable donor motivations of achievement, affiliation, philanthropy, and power relative to the dependent variable of the monetary donation level. The findings from this study suggest the donor motives of achievement and philanthropy significantly influence an individual donor's motivation to provide a monetary donation to a nonprofit when the donor did not have a previous relationship with the nonprofit organization but not a specific monetary donation level.

The results from this study suggest that affiliation and power motives are not predictive of different monetary donation levels. This research may support theory that focusing on the respective motivations of achievement and philanthropy of nonprofit donors might be justified in donor development campaigns. Strode (2006) theorized that motivations may assist a donor in deciding whether or not to provide or not provide a donation to a nonprofit, but motives do not determine the level of the monetary donation.

Research question 2. This research question was framed to explore if there is a statistical correlation between the motivation of achievement on the monetary donation level of a donor who did not have a previous relationship with the nonprofit. Achievement had the largest means score in the study and was statistically significant. McClelland (1961) defines achievement as an inner need or drive to achieve excellence. Staurowsky, Parkhouse, and Sachs (1996) referenced achievement as creating success factors such as loyalty and supporting the nonprofit, which both related to the success of the donor. Verner, Hecht, and Fansler (1998) also related the motive of achievement to factors associated with loyalty to the nonprofit and through the creation of tangible structures that will enable the nonprofit to achieve positive results. The results from this study provided evidence that donors may have provided a monetary donation to the basilica to seek new ways to grow the basilica's reputation, stature, and prominence throughout the world supporting the achievement motivation research findings of McClelland, Staurowsky et al., and Verner et al.

Strode (2006) determined achievement was the highest motivation by donor's who provided a monetary donation to a university's intercollegiate athletic department. The success achieved by a religious house of worship is not the same success typically associated with collegiate athletic competitions. However, Pope Benedict XVI recently bestowed the house of worship used in the study, previously a national shrine, the honorific title of a basilica in 2009.

The survey was sent to participants in 2010. The recent success and newness of becoming a named basilica by the Pope could have contributed to the high mean score as well as the significance and linear relationship for the achievement motivation within the study. Mahony et al. (2003) and Strode supported the achievement findings from their research as both r revealed donors were affected by factors related to success as evident with the statistically significant motive of achievement in this study.

Hypothesis 2. The null hypothesis was structured to outline there is no statistical correlation between the motivation of achievement relative to the level of the monetary donation. The alternative hypothesis was structured there is a statistical correlation between the motivation of achievement relative to the level of the monetary donation. The results allowed the acceptance of the alternative Hypotheses 2 that indicated a significant correlation in the monetary donation level based on different donor motivations unlike the achievement results discovered in Mahony et al. (2003) and Strode (2006). However, correlations and linear relationships between variables do not represent causation.

Research question 3. This research question was framed to explore if there is a statistical correlation between the motivation of affiliation on the monetary donation level of a donor who did not have a previous relationship with the nonprofit. The affiliation motive embraces donors gaining a sense of belonging with their peers that was problematic in this study of a nonprofit basilica serving guests and visitors on vacation. The participants in the study all reside outside the state of Florida and by function, had no previous relationship with the basilica as first time monetary donors. Strode (2006) stated that donors gain a community of affiliation in a multitude of ways but not limited to developing friendships with other donors and interacting with those who hold similar passions. The affiliation motivation is supported in the study by Strode with donors understanding their monetary donations are part of a larger effort to serve a basilica with other donors.

The Staurowsky et al. (1996) research resulted in a high mean score for the affiliation motivation. The results in this study are comparable to the Staurowsky et al. as the social motive in Staurowsky et al. centered on the need of affiliation and the ability to interact with others. Because participants had no previous relationship with the basilica as first time donors living outside Florida, the affiliation motivation may not have been important to the participants. However, those donors who did present a strong motivation of affiliation could have been motivated to be a part of something larger than themselves, understanding they were a part of similar and like-minded donors (Strode, 2006) supporting a basilica with people who shared similar experiences while visiting on vacation.

Hypothesis 3. The null hypothesis was structured to outline there is no statistical correlation between the motivation of affiliation relative to the level of the monetary donation. The alternative hypothesis was structured there is a statistical correlation between the motivation of affiliation relative to the level of the monetary donation. The results from this study allowed the acceptance of the null Hypotheses 3 as the results indicated no significant correlation in the monetary donation level based on different donor motivations like the affiliation results revealed in Mahony et al. (2003) and Strode (2006).

Research question 4. The research question was framed to explore if there is a statistical correlation between the motivation of philanthropy on the monetary donation level of a donor who did not have a previous relationship with the nonprofit. The philanthropic motivation to provide a monetary donation to the basilica was the most statistically significant of all of the variables in the study and earned the second highest mean score. The motive of philanthropy describes donors providing a monetary donation to a nonprofit with no thought of gaining personal benefits in return (Billing et al., 1985). The desire to help someone in need could have been a strong motive for participants in providing a monetary donation to a nonprofit like the basilica (Staurowsky et al., 1996). However, respective of the high mean score and statistical significance with the achievement motive in this study, there was evidence that participants who provided monetary support for philanthropic reasons may also have ulterior achievement motives suggesting the power motive (Verner et al., 1998).

Donor motivations of achievement and philanthropy are evidence in this study of donors having experienced a degree of self-satisfaction (Mahony et al., 2003) when providing a monetary donation because they believed providing support was a moral behavior so the basilica can achieve further success in the future (Strode, 2006). The results in the study mirrored prior research on philanthropy as a motive for providing monetary donations (Billing et al., 1985; Mahony et al., 2003; Staurowsky et al., 1996; Strode, 2006; Verner et al., 1998). Based on research, the philanthropy motive predicted to have a high mean score, as the results from the study illustrated the difference in providing a monetary donation to a nonprofit basilica based on the multiple theoretical motivational frameworks.

Explaining the results of philanthropy acquiring the second highest motivation by mean score, in addition to being the most significant motive based on the ANOVA, was that participants were donating to a Roman Catholic Basilica. Cascione (2000) described that religious beliefs were a vital role in motivation and donor philanthropy that contributed to the results of participants providing a monetary donation to a religious house of worship like the basilica in the study. Additionally, Andreoni (2006) offered the most important maxim to achieve fundraising goals was simply asking potential donors to contribute, the basilica requests

all visitors to support the mission of serving fellow guests who will visit after them that supports

this research finding.

The findings of the philanthropy motivation in the study supported the Ahlberg (1996)

research that examined motives of donors who provided a monetary donation to serve those

considered less fortunate and in most need of support. The basilica serving as the nonprofit

analyzed in this study hosts tourists and visitors attending a religious house of worship in

Florida. Serving as a host to tourists fits the biblical parable of the Good Samaritan that teaches

of being kind to those in need while traveling. The religious biblical reference provided

additional evidence of the philanthropy motivation results in this study. Cascione's (2000) and

Ahlberg findings on donor's religious beliefs and providing support to those in need of support

the philanthropy motivation results in this study.

However, the economic conditions in the United States addressed by Arcieri (2009)

established how the study's philanthropy results could be explained by the Weisbord and

DeScioli (2010) study that compared economic and psychological models of charitable helping

behaviors where donors put conditions on the monetary donation. Weisbord and DeScioli, and

Yuruk (2008) focused on the possible tax concerns, which were a relevant factor but not

necessarily reflected in the philanthropy and achievement motivation results from this study.

Even though the basilica is a religious house of worship, some of the participant donors may

have been motivated to provide a donation to improve their financial tax standing in a difficult

financial environment, although this statement was not asked in the survey.

The philanthropy motivation was apparent as the donor was personally committed to the

mission and vision of the specific nonprofit (Maynard, 2008). Individual donors in the United

States provided to beneficiaries such as the needy, the poor, educational institutions, religious organizations, and political candidates (Schortgen, 2006). The evidence from the data analysis in this study supported the findings of the motivations of philanthropy and charity developed by Cugliari (2005).

Even though large groups of individual donors provide monetary donations to a cause, the primary focus is assisting individuals in need (Cugliari, 2005). The results from the Cugliari (2005) study described the significant motivations of the donors in this study, as donor motivations of achievement and philanthropy were consistent with evidence from the research. Having the ability to describe the relationships between the results is important as Teraji (2009) stated the emotions and motivations could be useful for nonprofits to understand and meet the various needs of individual donors. The results from this study support the Olivola (2009 and Liu and Aaker (2008) research accepting the alternative hypothesis in this research. The authors illustrated that a donor who thought about charity, considered various ways of contributing, which included some amount of pain-effort. Few guests on vacation normally budget for philanthropic monetary donations to nonprofit organizations. Olivola (2009) and Liu and Aaker (2008) support the pain-effort in providing a monetary donation to a nonprofit like the basilica while on a vacation or traveling.

Hypothesis 4. The null hypothesis was structured to outline there is no statistical correlation between the motivation of philanthropy relative to the level of the monetary donation. The alternative hypothesis was structured there is a statistical correlation between the motivation of philanthropy relative to the level of the monetary donation. The results allowed the acceptance of the alternative Hypotheses 4 that indicated a significant correlation in the monetary donation level based on different donor motivations unlike the philanthropy results discovered in Mahony et al. (2003) and Strode (2006). However, correlations and linear relationships between variables do not represent causation.

Research question 5. This research question was framed to explore if there is a statistical correlation between the motivation of power on the monetary donation level of a donor who did not have a previous relationship with the nonprofit. Power had the lowest mean score of the motives used as an independent variable in this study. The power motive suggests a possible negative connotation or even a quid pro quo relationship with a nonprofit (Staurowsky et al., 1996). Strode (2006) maintained that providing a monetary donation is not explicitly based on quid pro quo. There is a basic expectation that when money is provided, individuals can have a say concerning decisions in exchange for their donations (Mahony et al., 2003). The power motive did not have a high mean score, as the motive is difficult to measure, as evident with past research (Verner et al., 1998).

One aspect could be the social acceptability of indicating a desire for power, as the perceived social foul may prohibit participants answering questions in a survey honestly despite the anonymous survey instrument. Donors often project donations as an altruistic gesture, rather than a selfish act for personal gain (Strode, 2006). The study mirrors other studies that additionally represented power to be the lowest motive, (Mahony et al., 2003; Staurowsky et al., 1996; Strode, 2006; Verner et al., 1998). However, the motive continually appears in donor survey instruments, as it seems that researchers must suspect that participants under report power as a true motive.

Hypothesis 5. The null hypothesis was structured to outline there is no statistical correlation between the motivation of power relative to the level of the monetary donation. The alternative hypothesis was structured there is a statistical correlation between the motivation of power relative to the level of the monetary donation. The results from this study allowed the acceptance of the null Hypotheses 5 as the results indicated no significant correlation in the monetary donation level based on different donor motivations like the power results revealed in Mahony et al. (2003) and Strode (2006).

Summary

The chapter outlined the results from this study as the data analysis provided evidence for the acceptance of the alternative Hypothesis 1. The alternative Hypothesis 1 stated there was a statistical difference among the four motives of achievement, affiliation, philanthropy, and power to provide a monetary donation based on the analysis of variance test. Observing the evidence provided from the data analysis of the mean score illustrated donor's highest motive to provide a monetary donation to the basilica was achievement, followed by philanthropy, affiliation, and power. The results from the single regression analysis allow the acceptance of the null Hypotheses 3 and 5, as there was no significant statistical correlation between the motivations of affiliation and power. The results from the single regression analysis allow the acceptance of the alternative Hypotheses 2 and 4, as there was a significant statistical correlation and linear relationship between the motivations of achievement and philanthropy.

The results from the ANOVA in this quantitative study supported the statistical significance of the donor motivations of achievement and philanthropy. The data analysis provided evidence to answer each of the respective research questions describing relationships between motivations of donors to provide a monetary donation to a nonprofit, which the individual donor had no previous relationship with the nonprofit based on the monetary donation level. The results from the single regression analysis implemented in this study suggest that achievement and philanthropy motivations maybe predictive of different monetary donation levels. However, correlations and linear relationships between variables of achievement and philanthropy do not represent causation. Incorporating theoretical frameworks, the statistical significance of the motives of achievement and philanthropy can offer evidence to describe the relationships of the motivations of donors providing a monetary donation to a nonprofit where there was no previous relationship with the donor.

CHAPTER 11: IMPLICATIONS, RECOMMENDATIONS, and CONCLUSIONS:

In a recessionary United States economy, current donors are decreasing monetary donations to nonprofit organizations (Arcieri, 2009). As a result, nonprofit organizations seek to attract new donors to replace the decreasing monetary donations by current nonprofit donors (Arcieri, 2009). Nonprofits must rethink development strategies to attract new donors as well as retain current donors (Durando, 2010). Understanding a donor's motivation to provide a monetary donation to a nonprofit is critical for the organization to achieve the necessary philanthropic monetary donations. Analysis on the motivations of donors who provide a monetary donation to a nonprofit without a previous relationship would assist nonprofits in their attempts to attract new donors. This study statistically analyzed the motivations of achievement, affiliation, philanthropy, and power of donors to provide a monetary donation to a nonprofit without having a previous relationship.

Research of donor motivations did not provide a singular and reliable motivational theoretical basis. Understanding a variety of motivational theories is necessary to describe relationships between different donor motivations to provide a monetary donation to a nonprofit when the donor did not have a previous relationship with a nonprofit. Motivational theory and the survey instrument implemented from the Strode (2006) research are applicable to describe the donor's motivation to provide a monetary donation to a nonprofit. Studies on philanthropic research theories associated with sales and marketing, integrated with motivation and religion philanthropic theories, provide explanations of motivations of donors to provide a monetary donation to a nonprofit. An investigation of multiple theoretical frameworks on motivational theory with research in philanthropy, motivation, and religion can help predict the motivation of a donor to provide a monetary donation to a nonprofit without a previous relationship with the nonprofit.

This quantitative study described the relationships between motivations of donors to provide a monetary donation to a nonprofit basilica without having a previous relationship with the nonprofit. This study incorporated, with permission, Strode's (2006) survey instrument that included multiple motivational theoretical frameworks to test donor motivations for providing monetary donations to a nonprofit. This study incorporated an analysis of four motives of achievement, affiliation, philanthropy, and power (independent variables) relative to the monetary donation level (dependent variable).

Strode's (2006) validated and reliable survey instrument was designed by Strode to minimize respondent error that established data collected from the survey were accurate and truthful based on quantitative research theory. Strode's (2006) study was focused on the creation of a psychometrically sound survey instrument based on motivational theory that can be used to create donor motivation profiles for nonprofit organizations. Strode's (2006) psychometrically valid quantitative survey instrument was sent to the target population of 484 donors who reside outside Florida and provided a monetary donation to a nonprofit basilica resulting in a sample of 216 participants. The nonprofit basilica in the study serves tourists and guests in a city in Florida as the target population included first time donors who did not have a previous relationship with the basilica.

This study incorporated quantitative statistical analysis to assist in the descriptions of the relationships between the donor motivations of achievement, affiliation, philanthropy, and power of donors who provided a monetary donation to a nonprofit without a previous relationship. The most suitable quantitative instrument to measure motives and demographics of a sample is a cross-sectional survey (Strode, 2006). According to Zikmund et al. (2009), a cross-sectional

survey instrument collects information from a sample at one data collection point from

participants. Strode provided written permission to use that survey instrument in this study. The

survey instrument was the main source of data collection that provided thorough data, which

assisted the descriptions of the attitudes and beliefs of a particular population (Lind et al., 2011).

A survey completed by the participants using Strode's (2006) psychometrically valid

quantitative survey instrument collected self-reported raw data to measure the individual donor's

motivations to provide a monetary donation to the basilica. Creswell (2009) stated the post-

positive worldview rejects or accepts the hypothesis in quantitative research. The post-positive

worldview was the most logical fit to test the respective hypotheses and answer each of the four

research questions in this study based on literature review, in addition to the Strode survey

instrument and research.

The quantitative survey instrument used for data collection facilitated the process for data

analysis to answer the respective research questions to describe the individual donor's

psychological motivations for providing a monetary donation to a nonprofit. The monetary

support of donors is critical for the organization's fundraising staff to achieve the necessary

philanthropic organizational funding. The quantitative research framework in this study on the

donor motivations of donors providing a monetary donation to a nonprofit where the donor had

no previous relationship is germane of the statistical data obtained from the donor participants

can directly benefit nonprofits. This study tested the data collected with used of a survey

instrument from the participants in the sample of the target population of donors living outside of

Florida who provided a monetary donation to the basilica.

The design of this study complied with the standards of conducting research with human participants set forth by Northcentral University. The researcher did not collect personal identification because the basilica did not want any identifiable demographic information on the surveys. The cover letter informed the participants that participation was voluntary. Participants in the target population could not participate by simply electing not to complete the survey. Assurances within the cover letter that accompanied the survey informed participants that no means were available to track identification or participation in the study. All participants who completed the survey would be anonymous.

The participants received a set of instructions within the cover letter in addition to the quantitative survey instrument to communicate instructions for their participation in this research study. The instructions included the directions of this research and the required information for addressing informed consent guidelines developed by Northcentral University's Internal Review Board (IRB). This study received approval from Northcentral University's IRB prior to any data collection.

The next sections of this final chapter will draw logical conclusions individually addressing each of the respective research questions and the null and alternative hypotheses from this study. This section will outline potential limitations in the interpretation of the results. This section will outline descriptions of the results fitting with the purpose and significance of this study. An implication of motivational theory based on the Strode (2006) research and survey instrument was applicable within the study to describe the donor's motivation to provide a monetary donation to a nonprofit where the donor had no previous relationship. The implications section will cover how the results fit with the purpose, significance, and existing literature focusing on philanthropy, motivation, and religion in philanthropy. Recommendations to fundraising staff at nonprofit organizations include incorporating accepted motivational theory to explain donor motivations when they create and maintain donor development campaigns. The study is an extension of philanthropic research within the development field on donor motivations, as the results applied to diverse nonprofits to determine donor motivations to provide a donation to a nonprofit without a previous relationship.

Implications

In a recessionary United States economy, current donors are decreasing monetary donations to nonprofit organizations (Arcieri, 2009). As a result, nonprofit organizations seek to attract new donors to replace the decreasing monetary donations by current nonprofit donors (Arcieri, 2009). Nonprofits must rethink development strategies to attract new donors as well as retain current donors (Durando, 2010). Understanding a donor's motivation to provide a monetary donation to a nonprofit is critical for the organization to achieve the necessary philanthropic monetary donations. Data on the motivations of donors who donate to a nonprofit without a previous relationship would assist nonprofits in their attempts to attract new donors. This research could additionally assist with the creation and development of new nonprofit organizations. Analysis on the motivations of donors who provide a monetary donation to a nonprofit without a previous relationship would assist nonprofits in their attempts to attract new donors. This study statistically analyzed the motivations of achievement, affiliation, philanthropy, and power of donors who provided a monetary donation to a nonprofit without having a previous relationship relative to the monetary donation level.

Research question 1. The research question was framed to explore if there was a statistical difference of the variance among the four motives of achievement, affiliation, philanthropy, and power relative to the level of the monetary donation. Numerous philanthropic and donor development studies have offered donor motivations are related providing a monetary donation to a nonprofit organization. The studies outlined in this research have not analyzed this motivational relationship relative to providing a monetary donation based on a monetary donation level. Two studies (Mahony et al., 2003; Strode, 2006) have empirically tested the relationship of the motivations of donors providing a monetary donation to a nonprofit. Similar to the research questions incorporated in this study, Mahony et al., 2003 and Strode, 2006 revealed no significant differences in the monetary donation level to a nonprofit based on the donor motivations. This study fits into the knowledge base of philanthropic business development as it adds new knowledge of motivations of donors providing a monetary donation to a nonprofit when there was not a previous relationship with the nonprofit organization.

Hypothesis 1. The null hypothesis was structured there is no statistical difference of the variance among the four motivations of achievement, affiliation, philanthropy, and power relative to the level of the monetary donation. The alternative hypothesis was structured there is a statistical difference among the four motivations of achievement, affiliation, philanthropy, and power relative to the level of the monetary donation. Acceptance of the alternative Hypothesis 1 in this study is because of the difference among the four motives of achievement, affiliation, philanthropy, and power.

The data analysis from the responses of the mean scores illustrated the donor's highest motive to provide a monetary donation to the basilica was achievement, followed by philanthropy, affiliation, and power. The results from the ANOVA in the quantitative study represented the donor motivations of achievement and philanthropy were statistically significant for donors to provide a monetary donation but not on the specific monetary donation level. The findings from this analysis support the Strode (2006) study that also revealed achievement as significant for donors to provide a monetary donation. The statistical significance of the motives of achievement and philanthropy could describe the relationships of the motivations of participants providing a monetary donation to a nonprofit without a previous relationship with the donor but not the respective monetary donation level.

The null Hypothesis 1 supported donor motivations having no effect on donors providing a monetary donation to a nonprofit based on the monetary donation level. However, this study is unique by accepting the null Hypothesis 1 that offers there is a difference in the variance of the motivations influencing a donor to provide a monetary donation to a nonprofit. This offers a significant result of the achievement and philanthropy motivations to this research. The significance of rejecting the null Hypothesis 1 suggests that different motives of achievement, affiliation, philanthropy, and power are predictive of donors providing a monetary donation to a nonprofit without a previous relationship but not predictive of different monetary donation levels.

This research finding may not justify a significant focus on the motivations of donors relative to the monetary donation level in future research. Motivations could be influential donors deciding whether or not to provide or not provide a monetary donation to a nonprofit, however, this conclusion cannot be determined without surveying non-donors, which is a limitation of this study. This study provided new evidence to suggest that different donor motivations of providing a monetary donation to a nonprofit when the donor did not have a previous relationship do not determine the monetary donation level but influence the achievement and philanthropy motivation to provide a donation in any amount.

Nonprofit organizations can use the results from this study to design campaigns to attract new donors as well as maintaining monetary donations of current donors. Development staff at nonprofit organizations must create and design development strategies because in the current economy, many donors are not providing a monetary donation because of financial constraints. The executives and fundraising staff at nonprofit organization must understand an individual's psychological motivation to supply financial support for the organization's fundraising staff to achieve necessary philanthropic organizational funding.

Research questions 2-5. These research questions were framed to explore if there is a statistical correlation with the respective motivations of achievement, affiliation, philanthropy, and power on the monetary donation level of a donor who did not have a previous relationship with the nonprofit.

Research question 2. The research question was framed to explore if there is a statistical correlation between the motivation of achievement on the monetary donation level of a donor who did not have a previous relationship with the nonprofit. The motive of achievement had the highest mean score in this study and was statistically significant. The results have a basis within theoretical frameworks adding new knowledge to the business development field by providing information that explains donor motivation providing a monetary donation to a nonprofit with no previous relationship with the donor. The statistical results from answering this research question did provide a linear relationship after the single regression analysis.

McClelland (1961) defined the motivation of achievement as a motivation of an inner need, or drive, to achieve excellence. Staurowsky, Parkhouse, and Sachs (1996) referenced achievement as creating success factors such as loyalty and supporting the nonprofit organizations. Both factors relate to the success of the donor as the results indicate donors want the basilica to achieve success. Verner, Hecht, and Fansler (1998) stated achievement aligns to factors associated with loyalty to the nonprofit and through the creation of tangible structures that will enable the nonprofit to achieve positive results. The achievement motivation maintains the donor more involved with the organization creating a customer-like relationship supporting customer relationships driver theories supported by Lacey (2007) and Waters (2007). The research significance from this study provided data to explain the purpose of the study as the basilica donors seek achievement to assist with new ways to grow the basilica's reputation, stature, and prominence throughout the world.

Research question 3. The research question was framed to explore if there is a statistical correlation between the motivation of affiliation on the monetary donation level of a donor who did not have a previous relationship with the nonprofit. The affiliation motive embraces donors gaining a sense of belonging with their peers that was problematic in this study of a nonprofit basilica serving guests and visitors on vacation. The participants in the study all reside outside the state of Florida and by function, had no previous relationship with the basilica as first time monetary donors. Strode (2006) stated that donors gain a community of affiliation in a multitude of ways but not limited to developing friendships with other donors and interacting with those who hold similar passions. The affiliation motivation is supported in the study by Strode (2006) with donors understanding their monetary donations are part of a larger effort to serve a basilica with other donors. The statistical results from answering this research question did not provide a linear relationship after the single regression analysis.

Research Question 4. The research question was framed to explore if there is a statistical correlation between the motivation of philanthropy on the monetary donation level of a donor who did not have a previous relationship with the nonprofit. The results in the study mirrored prior research on philanthropy as a motive for providing monetary donations to a nonprofit (Billing et al., 1985; Mahony et al., 2003; Staurowsky et al., 1996; Strode (2006);

Verner et al., 1998). Based on previous research within philanthropy motivation, there was

expectation of the philanthropy motive to have a high mean score, but the current study is

significant meeting the purpose in understanding motivations providing a monetary donation to a

nonprofit with no previous relationship. The statistical results from answering this research

question did provide a linear relationship after the single regression analysis.

Locke (2002) contended that Frankl (1984) revealed that meaning is the basic human

motivation accomplished through suffering, self-sacrifice, and taking a stand toward conditions.

Locke's research supposed that motivation was more than merely alleviating suffering, as service

in the church provided more meaning in life than only weekly church attendance that makes the

study significant as it describes motivations in providing a monetary donation to the basilica with

no previous relationship. The research significance of the philanthropic motive results fit the

purpose of the research describing relationships for donors with no previous relationship to a

nonprofit. The philanthropy motive earned the second highest mean score and was the most

statistically significant of all of the variables used in the study. The motive of philanthropy

describes donors providing a monetary donation to a nonprofit with no thought of gaining

personal benefits in return supported by human motivational theories by Maslow (1943) and

Bandura (1986).

Cascione (2000) described that religious beliefs were a vital role in motivation and donor

philanthropy, which contributed to the results of participants providing a monetary donation to a

religious house of worship like the Catholic basilica because providing a monetary donation is a

right behavior. Strong donor motivations of achievement and philanthropy were evident as

donors received a self-satisfactory emotion when providing a monetary donation because they

thought it was a moral behavior, so the basilica can achieve future success. The Ahlberg (1996) study supported the results where the majority of church members in one independent congregation provided a monetary donation to causes that benefited the donor directly, as other donors provided a monetary donation to serve those considered less fortunate and in most need of support as donors to the basilica wanted to assist future visitors like themselves.

Research question 5. The research question was framed to explore if there is a statistical correlation between the motivation of power on the monetary donation level of a donor who did not have a previous relationship with the nonprofit. Power had the lowest mean score of the motives used as an independent variable in this study. The power motive suggests a possible negative connotation or even a quid pro quo relationship with a nonprofit (Staurowsky et al., 1996). Strode (2006) maintained that providing a monetary donation is not explicitly based on quid pro quo. There is a basic expectation that when money is provided to a nonprofit, individuals can have a say concerning decisions in exchange for their donations (Mahony et al., 2003). The power motive did not have a high mean score, as the motive is difficult to measure, as evident with past research (Verner et al., 1998). The statistical results from answering this research question did not provide a linear relationship after the single regression analysis.

Hypotheses 2-5. The Hypotheses 2-5 from this study postulated the null hypothesis there are no statistical correlations with the respective donor motivations of achievement, affiliation, philanthropy, and power relative to level of the monetary donation. The alternative Hypotheses 2-5 stated there are statistical correlations with the respective motives achievement, affiliation, philanthropy, and power relative to level of the monetary donation.

The results from the single regression analysis allow the acceptance of the null Hypotheses 3 and 5, as there was no statistical correlation in the data with the variables of affiliation and power. This study results permits acceptance of the alternative Hypotheses 2 and

4, as the results from the single regression analysis denoted a linear relationship between the significant motives of achievement and philanthropy on the monetary donation but not the monetary donation level. The data from the single regression analysis indicated the donor's monetary donation were likely to be influenced by the achievement and philanthropy motivations.

The significant motivations would be critical for nonprofit organization's future development campaigns. The positive linear relationship from the single regression analysis of the achievement and philanthropy motivations indicated correlation but not causation. The results from the single regression analysis suggest the motives of affiliation and power did not predict any significant variance in the level of the monetary donation.

Previous research has implied that motivations are related to nonprofit donor's monetary donation levels however, these studies have not tested this relationship. Previous research indicated that Mahony et al. (2003) and Strode (2006) empirically tested this relationship between donor motivations and monetary donation levels. Both Mahony et al. (2003) and Strode (2006) discovered no significant correlations in monetary donation level based on different motives achievement, affiliation, philanthropy, and power. The results from this study allowed the acceptance of the null Hypotheses 3 and 5 as the results indicated no significant correlations in the monetary donation level based on different donor motivations like the results discovered in Mahony et al. (2003) and Strode (2006).

However, this study can accept the alternative Hypotheses 2 and 4, as the results from the single regression analysis denoted the motivations of achievement, and philanthropy did express a linear relationship between the significant motives of achievement and philanthropy and the level of the monetary donation. The results from this study suggest that motivations of achievement and philanthropy are significant, which did not occur when compared to the results of Mahony et al. (2003) and Strode (2006). This research may support theory that focusing on the respective motivations of nonprofit donors might not be fully justified in donor development campaigns expect possibly the motivations of achievement and philanthropy to influence monetary donation levels.

Strode (2006) theorized that motivations may assist a donor in deciding whether to provide or not provide a monetary donation to a nonprofit, but motives do not determine the level of the monetary donation. Research on donor motivations with a focus on why donors provide a monetary donation to a nonprofit did not provide an apparent and reliable motivational theoretical basis. Comprehending a variety of motivational theories is necessary to describe the complete relationships between donor motivations providing a monetary donation to a nonprofit. The basis for a multiple theoretical understanding was germane where the donor had no previous relationship with a nonprofit.

Motivational theory based on the Strode (2006) research and Strode survey instrument was applicable within the study to describe the donor's motivation to provide a monetary donation to a nonprofit where the donor had no previous relationship. Integration of research from motivation and religion philanthropic theories provide frameworks for the respective research questions to identify which motivation compels an individual to provide a monetary donation to a specific nonprofit. An investigation of the multiple theoretical frameworks on motivational theory along with research within philanthropy, motivation, and religion research can suggest the motives of donors providing a monetary donation with no previous relationship with the donor and nonprofit.

Limitations. Limitations of this study include the participants self-reporting data collected through the survey instrument. Participants who completed the questionnaire could misinterpret the questions in the survey. The assumption of the validity of the participant's mailing addresses provided by the basilica could have limited this study. Because the donors provided a monetary donation to the basilica within the past calendar year, the address provided by the basilica for the research was likely accurate, thus increasing the response rate. This study only included participants who were first time donors not having a previous relationship with the basilica in attempt to answer each of the respective research questions in this study. The results from this study could have been limited by not surveying donors with an established relationship with the nonprofit basilica.

Limitations of the study included the basilica wanting to protect the identity of its donors. The basilica did not permit gender identification and other demographic information included within the study's survey instrument. Having gender and other demographic information as variables for future research would provide deeper understanding of a potential donor profile to provide a monetary donation to a nonprofit organization. Additionally, the personal or household income level of the donors would have been beneficial in the analysis of this study. Ideally, the income of donors would need to be controlled to account for the results from this study to further test the effect on the specific monetary donation levels.

The data collected to conduct the ANOVA in this study are from one unique sample from one specific nonprofit organization within the United States. This study surveyed a target population from one nonprofit institution where participants only responded to the provided survey questions and were not able to elaborate on the survey instrument. Utilizing one nonprofit organization made it difficult to generalize the results to dissimilar nonprofit entities seeking to gain knowledge on donor motivations providing a monetary donation to a nonprofit. The nonprofit basilica is ideal for this study because the basilica met the characteristics of first time donors having no previous relationship with a nonprofit organization.

The nonprofit basilica did not permit any demographic information collection of participants in this study. The basilica wanted to ensure the anonymity of their donors serving as participants in this research study. Non-response bias considers the answers of participants are different from the potential answers of the target population who did not respond. Some participant donors from the target population in this study could have not responded to the survey because of the expectations of future donations with a survey response. A donor having a genuinely positive experience when visiting the basilica would be the most ideal to complete and respond to the survey in this study. Conversely, a donor having a positive experience visiting during a vacation could have felt disconnected from the basilica after returning to their home to complete and respond to the survey on their motivations to provide a monetary donation.

Females typically plan family vacations, as an assumption, thus mothers and grandmothers would be most likely to complete and respond to the survey based on visiting the basilica and providing a first time monetary donation to the nonprofit basilica. Additional non-response bias could have occurred, as participants may have felt pressured to inflate or deflate their actual monetary donation level because of the expectations of future donor expectations so they chose not to participate. Participants could also have felt embarrassed with their actual monetary donation amount and elected not to participate in the survey. Participants who provided larger monetary donation amounts could have elected not to participate in the survey because of perceived requests for increased monetary donations in the future.

This study's purpose and significance fit with research literature focusing on philanthropy, motivation, and religion in philanthropy. Research literature helps describe the relationships between donor motives and subsequent monetary donation in which the individual donor had no previous relationship with the nonprofit based on the level of donation. The comprehension of philanthropy, human motivation, and religion's role in philanthropy, as it related to altruistic behaviors in practice and historical significance is important to this study.

The examination of literature on customer relationship frameworks in philanthropy, motivation, and the role of religion in philanthropy, presented how the sub-topics, typically associated with traditional business marketing endeavors. The research significance extends to donors and nonprofits having a traditional customer and for-profits business relationship while appealing to altruistic motivations as providing monetary donations is a correct behavior. The history of philanthropy in the United States in literature focused on both the individual donor as well as the philosophical understandings of nonprofit organizations, which highlighted research about the ways modern philanthropy operates like for-profit businesses.

The philanthropy motive assimilated theoretical frameworks associated with sales and marketing. These theories described motivational theories of providing monetary donations to a nonprofit. The motivation section outlined the psychological understandings of the human motivation of altruistic helping behaviors that used multiple motivational theory frameworks. An analysis of research in the psychology of human motivation field, showed parallels that illustrated why individuals donate to philanthropic institutions and causes. The religion in philanthropy section explored donors providing monetary donations in religion and highlighted recent research in the analysis of donor motivations in religious congregations and contexts.

Recommendations

This section of the chapter will outline the recommendations for future research and describe how new knowledge was introduced in the fields of philanthropy and business development. Executives and fundraising staff at nonprofit organizations should incorporate accepted motivational theory to explain donor motivations for donor development campaigns. The study is an extension of philanthropic research within the development field on donor motivations, as the results applied to diverse nonprofit organizations. Future research could observe similar religious houses of worship and donor motivations where another researcher may provide consistent measureable outcomes incorporated by development offices in fundraising campaigns.

The mean score data was interpreted that participants were inspired by the achievement and philanthropic motivations respectively to provide monetary support to the basilica above the other motivations of affiliation and power. Because the achievement and philanthropy motives were the most significant from the ANOVA respectively, all development promotional materials from the basilica should highlight recent accomplishments, such as elevation to a basilica status, while stressing that donations help to ensure future achievement because serving others is a right and good behavior. The basilica development office has limited control over initiatives directed from the Catholic Church in Rome, or the local Catholic diocese. However, the development staff needs to communicate the benefits of altruistic behavior, completion of successful projects, and events occurring at the basilica to donors.

One aspect of fundraising development is the basilica does not take advantage is online donations. Gaulke (2010) conducted research on the motivations of current and first-time online donors where significant relationships with both groups for the commitment and performance of the organization. The Gaulke research supported the findings from this research as it also supported the motivation of achievement with the highest mean score and was statistically significant. The basilica could increase donors' motivation to provide monetary donations if the organization embraced an online platform for current and future donors appealing to the achievement motive.

Development professionals at other nonprofits need to comprehend social, economic, and political demands as well as discover common decision-making methods associated with altruistic behavior while operating under a successful business model of success and achievement. The results indicate the basilica, like other nonprofit and charitable organizations, should focus on motivating donors to increase donation levels, as 93.5% of all participants provided less than $399. The concern is a common issue particularly in a sensitive United States economy, for all profit and nonprofit businesses. At a nonprofit organization, the employees must understand the differences between the donors of various nonprofits. The research can assist development officers so they can develop campaigns that maximize contributions in development campaigns based on an increased knowledge of their donors.

Another study could offer further insight into donor motivations were an analysis could compare the results of the donor motivations from when the house of worship used in this study was a named shrine. Comparisons of the results from donors providing a monetary donation to shrine and then to the basilica could then be compared with the results from this study. Implementing the survey instrument is germane to conduct tests and analyze results from other houses of worship to draw further conclusions. Comparing the results of the survey conducted at other religious houses of worship, such as other Christian denominations, a Jewish Synagogue, or a Buddhist temple would provide further insights to donor motivations. The test would determine if an affiliation with specific religions had an impact on motivation respective of the donation level. The basilica wanted to protect the identity of its donors, and did not permit gender identification or other demographic information collected with the study's survey instrument. Gender as a variable in future research would provide further knowledge to create and implement campaigns based on a donor profile.

Other studies based on the research could analyze the donor motivations from other Catholic basilicas. Then, a comparison of motivations in unique donor situations, other than having no previous relationship, possibly creates a donor profile for Catholic basilicas. By extension, the findings apply to local parishes as well (some basilicas are local parishes). Using the same basilica from the study is ideal for future research testing the motives from donors living in the state of Florida in comparison to donors' motivations with no previous relationship. A researcher could conduct qualitative research through personal interviews with participants who reside both in and out of Florida that would gain further insights into donor motivations, particularly an analysis of the power motivation that others' philanthropic research support underrepresentation.

Last, the research replicated at the basilica during a non-recession period within the United States economy could show different results from the current study. Future replication could determine if the current United States recession was a factor in the research study's findings. The replication could additionally divulge further evidence if the economic recession had an effect on donor motivations in providing a monetary donation to a nonprofit.

Conclusion

The final chapter of this study contained the comparative quantitative analysis and reviewed the components of the research, provided a brief description of the findings, and recommendations for the future based on the research study. The implications of the results from the ANOVA indicate relationships between the statistically significant motivations of achievement and philanthropy and subsequent monetary donation to a nonprofit, which the individual donor had no previous relationship. Critical analysis addressed the recommendations for future research adding new knowledge to business development and philanthropic research. Recommendations from the statistical significance of the motives of achievement and philanthropy indicated that motives should appear in all development and promotional materials from the basilica that highlight recent accomplishments (achievement) and share why providing a monetary donation is a positive behavior and correct choice to make (philanthropy).

Analysis of the implications from the research describes relationships between donor motives and subsequent monetary donation, and finally offers recommendations for future use and research. An implication of motivational theory based on the Strode (2006) research and survey instrument was applicable within the study to describe the donor's motivation to provide a monetary donation to a nonprofit where the donor had no previous relationship but not on the specific monetary donation level. The implications section in this chapter highlighted the results from this study aligned with the purpose, significance, and existing literature from this research study. Recommendations to fundraising staff at nonprofit organizations include incorporating accepted motivational theory to explain donor motivations when they create and maintain donor development campaigns. The study is an extension of philanthropic research within the development field on donor motivations, as the results applied to diverse nonprofit organizations.

The philanthropy motive assimilated theoretical frameworks associated with sales and marketing and was important as it described motivational theories of donors providing a monetary donation to a nonprofit. The motivation section outlined the psychological understandings of the human motivation of altruistic helping behaviors that used multiple motivational theory frameworks. An analysis of research in the psychology of human motivation field, demonstrated parallels that illustrated why individuals provide monetary donations to philanthropic institutions and causes. The religion in philanthropy section of the chapter explored why donors provide monetary donations to religious nonprofits and highlighted recent research in the analysis of donor motivations in providing monetary donations to religious congregations.

Future research could observe similar religious houses of worship and donor motivations where another researcher may provide consistent measurable outcomes incorporated by development offices in fundraising campaigns. Development professionals at other nonprofits need to comprehend social, economic, and political demands as well as discover common decision-making methods associated with altruistic behavior while operating under a successful business model of success and achievement. Future replication of the study could determine if the current United States recession was a factor in the research study's findings. The replication could additionally divulge further evidence if the economic recession had an effect on donor motivations in providing a monetary donation to a nonprofit.

CHAPTER 12: REFERENCES

Arcieri, K. (2009, July 5). Nonprofit groups sharpen fundraising strategies in recession. *McClatchy Business News*. Retrieved from http://mcclatchy.com

Ahlberg, R. H. (1996). My fellow camels: A ministry project on stewardship and philanthropy in a wealthy and privileged congregation. (Doctoral dissertation). Retrieved from ProQuest Digital Dissertations. (AAT No. 9803440)

Allport, G. W. (1966). The religious context of prejudice. *Journal for the Scientific Study of Religion. 5*, 447-457. doi:10.2307/1384172

Andreoni, J. (2006). Leadership giving in charitable fund-raising. *Journal of Public Economic Theory. 8,* 1-22. doi:10.1111/j.1467-9779.2006.00250.x

Andreoni, J., & Payne, A. A. (2003). Do government grants to private charities crowd out giving or fund-raising? *American Economic Review. 93*, 792-812. doi:10.1257/000282803322157098

Anft, M., & Lipman, H. (2003). How Americans give. *Chronicle of Philanthropy. 15*(4), 6-9. Retrieved from http://philanthropy.com

Bandura, A. (1986). *Social foundations of thought and action: A social cognitive.* Englewood Cliffs, NJ: Prentice Hall.

Barnes, M. L. (2006). Reducing donor fatigue syndrome. *Nonprofit World. 24*(2), 8-9. Retrieved from http://nonprofitworld.org

Bendapudi, N., Singh, S., & Bendapudi, V. (1996). Enhancing helping behavior: An integrative framework for promotion planning. *Journal of Marketing. 60*, 33-49. doi:10.2307/1251840

Biddle, W. W. (1953). *The cultivation of community leaders: Up from the grass roots.* New York, NY: Harper and Brothers.

Billing, J., Holt, D., & Smith, J. (1985). *Athletic fund-raising: Exploring the motives behind private donations*. Chapel Hill, NC: University of North Carolina Press.

Birch, D., & Veroff, J. (1966). *Motivation: A study of action.* Belmont, CA: Brooks/Cole Publishing Company.

Boorstin, D. J. (1987). *Hidden history*. New York, NY: Harper and Row.

Bradley, B., Jansen, P., & Silverman, J. (2003). The non-profit sector's $100 billion opportunity. *Harvard Business Review. 81*, 94-108. Retrieved from http://hbr.org

Bremner, R. H. (1996). *Giving: Charity and philanthropy in history.* New Brunswick, NJ: Transaction Publishers.

Bryant, W. K., Jeon-Slaughter, H., Kang, H., & Tax, A. (2003). Participation in philanthropic activities: Donating money and time. *Journal of Consumer Policy. 26*, 43-73. doi:10.1023/A:10022626529603

Burton, A. L. (2010). Motivations to give back: Attributes of professional football players who support nonprofit organizations. (Doctoral dissertation). Retrieved from ProQuest Digital Dissertations. (AAT No. 3412234)

Cascione, G. L. (2000). Religion, motivation, and philanthropy to higher education. (Doctoral dissertation). Retrieved from ProQuest Digital Dissertations. (AAT No. 9977130)

Charity Navigator (2007, May 1). *2007 Special Events Study.* Retrieved from http://www.charitynavigator.org/index.cfm?bay=studies.events

Chelladurai, P. (1999). *Human resource management in sport and recreation.* Champaign, IL: Human Kinetics.

Cohen, J. (1992). A power primer. *Psychological Bulletin, 112*(1), 155-159. doi: 10.1037/0033-2909.112.1.155

Council on Foundations (2000). *An abbreviated history of the philanthropy tradition in the United States.* Retrieved from www.cof.org/whatis/history/history.htm

Creswell, J. W. (2009). *Research design: Qualitative, quantitative, and mixed method approaches* (3rd ed.). Thousand Oaks, CA: Sage Publications.

Cugliari, C. W. (2005). A post-positivist qualitative study of philanthropic donors to Appalachian Ohio. (Doctoral dissertation). Retrieved from ProQuest Digital Dissertations. (AAT No. 3180124)

Cunningham, B., & Cochi-Ficano, C. (2002). The determinants of donative revenue flows from alumni of higher education. *Journal of Human Resources. 37*, 540-570. doi:10.2307/3069681

Dawes, C. T., Fowler, J. H., Johnson, T., Mc Elreath, R., & Smirnov, O. (2007). Egalitarian motives in humans. *Nature. 446*, 794-797. doi:10.1038/nature05651

Dillman, D. (2000). *Mail and internet surveys.* New York, NY: Wiley and Sons.

Durando, J. (2010, November 17). Americans plan to maintain their level of charitable giving. *USA Today.* Retrieved from http://usatoday.com

Ehrenberg, R., & Smith, C. (2001). *The sources and uses of annual giving at private research universities*. Retrieved from http://digitalcommons.ilr.cornell.edu/cgi/viewcontent.cgi?article=1023&context=working papers

Erdfelder, E., Faul, F., & Buchner, A. (1996). GPOWER: A general power analysis program. *Behavior Research Methods, Instruments, & Computers, 28*, 1-11.

Estes, W. K. (1991). *Statistical models in behavioral research*. Philadelphia, PA: Lawrence Erlbaum Associates, Inc.

Feingold, M. (1987). Philanthropy, pomp, and patronage: Historical reflections upon the endowment of culture. *Daedalus. 116*(1), 155-177. Retrieved from http://mitpress.mit.edu/daedalus

Frankl, V. (1984). *Man's search for meaning*. New York, NY: Simon and Schuster, Inc.

Friedrichs, R. W. (1960). Alter versus ego: An exploratory assessment of altruism. *American Sociological Review. 25*, 496-508. doi:10.2307/2092934

Furnham, A., & Argyle, M. (1998). *The psychology of money*. New York, NY: Routledge.

Gaulke, K. R. (2010). Motivation factors of current and first-time online donors. (Doctoral dissertation). Retrieved from ProQuest Digital Dissertations. *(AAT No. 3432500)*

Gray, P. (1994). *Psychology*. New York, NY: Worth Publishers.

Grimm, R. T. (2002). From retail to wholesale giving. *Foundation News and Commentary, 43*(5), 26. Retrieved from http://foundationnews.org

Gross, R. A. (2003). Giving in America: From charity to philanthropy. In L. J. Freidman & M.D. McGarvie (Eds.), *Charity, philanthropy, and civility in American history (29-48)*. Cambridge, MA: Cambridge University Press.

Guy, B., & Patton, W. (1989). The Marketing of altruistic causes: Understanding why people help. *Journal of Consumer Marketing. 6*, 19-30. doi:10.1108/EUM0000000002536

Harwell, M. R., & Gatti, G. G. (2001). Rescaling ordinal data to interval data in educational research. *Review of Educational Research. 7*, 105-131. doi:10.3102/00346543071001105

Henke, L. L., & Fontenot, G. (2009). Why give to charity: How motivations for giving predict types of causes supported. *Allied Academies International Conference, Academy of Marketing Studies. 14*(1), 16-17.

Herzberg, F., Mausner, B., & Snyderman, B. (1959). *The motivation to work*. New York, NY:

Wiley.

Hibbert, S., & Horne, S. (1996). Giving to charity: Questioning the donor decision process. *Journal of Consumer Marketing. 13*, 4-13. doi:10.1108/07363769610115366

High, R. (2000, Summer). Important factors in designing statistical power analysis studies: The size of your study sample is critical to producing meaningful results. *Computing News.* Retrieved from http://cc.uoregon.edu/cnews/summer2000/

Hoffman, M. (2008). The best cause of all. *Inc. 30*(6), 23-24. Retrieved from http://inc.com

Jacobs, F., & Marudas, N. (2006), Excessive, optimal, and insufficient fundraising among the Nonprofit Times 100. *International Journal of Nonprofit and Voluntary Sector Marketing. 11*, 105-114. doi:10.1002/nvsm.46

Johnston, L. F. (2002). Maximizing donor value: Key satisfaction drivers for major donors to nonprofit organizations. (Doctoral dissertation). Retrieved from ProQuest Digital Dissertations. *(*AAT No.3059656)

Karl, B. D., & Katz, S. N. (1987). Foundations and ruling class elites. *Daedalus, 116*(1), 1-40. Retrieved from http://mitpress.mit.edu/daedalus

Kelly, K. (1991). *Fund raising and public relations: A critical analysis*. Hillsdale, NJ: Lawrence Erlbaum.

Khanna, J., Posnett, J., & Sandler, T. (1995). Charity donations in the UK: New evidence based on panel data. *Journal of Public Economics. 56*, 257-272. doi:10.1016/00472727(94)01421-J

Klebanow, S., & Lowenkopf, E. (1991). *Money and mind*. New York, NY: Plenum Press.

Kottasz, R. (2003). How should charitable organizations motivate young professionals to give philanthropically? *International Journal of Nonprofit and Voluntary Sector Marketing. 9*, 9-27. doi:10.1002/nvsm.230

Lacey, R. (2007). Relationship drivers of customer commitment. *Journal of Marketing Theory and Practice. 15*, 315-334. doi:10.2753/MTP1069-6679150403

Lackie, M. B. (2010). Alumni giving at Arkansas Tech University: College experiences and motivations to give as predictors of giving behavior. (Doctoral Dissertation). Retrieved from ProQuest Digital Dissertations. (AAT 3438055)

Locke, J. K. (2002). Self-transcendence in relation to self-actualization and the effect on motivation in the church. (Doctoral Dissertation). Retrieved from ProQuest Digital Dissertations. (AAT No.3050699)

Love, T., & Higgins, C. (2007). Do we know enough about corporate philanthropy?
    The Journal of Corporate Citizenship. 27, 18-21. Retrieved from http://www.greenleaf-
    publishing.com

Lind, D.A., Marchal, W.G., & Wathen, S.A. (2011) *Statistical techniques in business and
    economics* (15th ed.). New York, NY: McGraw-Hill Companies, Inc.

Liu, W., & Aaker, J. (2008). The happiness of giving: The time-ask effect. *Journal of Consumer
    Research. 35*, 543-557. doi:10.1086/588699

Mahony, D., Gladden, J., & Funk, D. (2003). Examining athletic donors at NCAA
    division I institutions. *International Sports Journal. 7*(1), 9-27.

Maimonides, M. (1979). *The code of Maimonides*. New Haven, CT: Yale University Press.

Maslow, A. (2009). *Father of modern management and leadership by employee motivation.*
    Retrieved from http://www.abrahammaslow.com

Maslow, A. (1943). A theory of human motivation. *Psychological Review. 50*, 370-396.
    doi:10.1037/h0054346

Maynard, G. F. (2008). Philanthropy is not asking for a favor, it is giving a favor. *Frontiers of
    Health Services Management. 24*(4), 31-35. Retrieved from http://ache.org

McClelland, D. (1975). *Power: The inner experience*. New York, NY: Wiley.

McClelland, D. (1961). *The achieving society*. Princeton, NJ: D. Van Nostrand Company.

McClelland, D., Davis, W., Kalin, R., & Wanner, E. (1972). *The drinking man.* New York, NY:
    The Free Press.

McCully, G. (2000). Is this a paradigm shift? *Foundation News and Commentary. 2*(41), 20-22.
    Retrieved from http://foundationnews.org

McKinley-Floyd, L., & Shrestha, N. (2008). Segmentation strategies for non-profits: Mining the
    emerging market of black gold. *Journal of Business and Industrial Marketing. 23*(6),
    416-428. doi: 10.1108/08858620810894463

Miller, L. A. (2008). A case study on the reasons females make charitable donations. (Doctoral
    dissertation). Retrieved from ProQuest Digital Dissertations. *(*AAT No. 3357435)

Morino, M. (2000, March). *Completing the wealth cycle in the new economy.* Presented at the
    Greater Washington Business Philanthropy Summit, Washington, D.C. Retrieved from
    http://morino.org/advan_sp_cyc.asp

Okten, C., & Weisbrod B. A. (2000). Determinants of donations in private non-profit markets. *Journal of Public Economics. 75*, 255-272. doi:10.1016/S0047-2727(99)00066-3

Okunade, A., & Berl, R. (1997). Determinants of charitable giving of business school alumni. *Research in Higher Education. 38*, 201-214. doi:10.1023/A:1024933720131

Olsen, S., & Galimidi, B. (2009). Managing social and environmental impact: A new discipline for a new economy. *Brown Journal of World Affairs. 15*(2), 43-56. doi: 10.1596/978-0-821-36179-5

Olivola, C. Y. (2009). The martyrdom effect: When the prospect of suffering for a cause increases contributions to the cause. (Doctoral dissertation). Retrieved from ProQuest Digital Dissertations. (AAT No. 3356737)

Ott, S. J. (2001). *The nature of the nonprofit sector.* Boulder, CO: Westview Press.

Peifer, J.L. (2010). The economics and sociology of religious giving: Instrumental rationality or communal bonding? *Social Forces. 88*(4), 1569-1594. doi: 10.1353/sof.2010.0004

Prugsamatz, R. (2010). The learning organization. *Bradford. 17*, 243. doi:10.1108/09696471011034937

Rennie, D. L. (2008). Two thoughts on Abraham Maslow. *The Journal of Humanistic Psychology. 48*, 445-449. doi:10.1177/0022167808320537

Sargeant, A., & Woodliffe, L. (2007). Gift giving: An interdisciplinary review. *International Journal of Nonprofit and Sector Marketing. 12*, 275-308. doi:10.1002/nvsm.308

Sargent, A. (1999). Charitable giving: Towards a model of donor behavior. *Journal of Marketing Management. 15*, 215-238. doi:10.1362/026725799784870351

Schneedwind, J. B. (1996). *Giving: Western ideas of philanthropy.* Bloomington: IN University Press.

Schervish, P. G., & Havens J. J. (1997). Social participation and charitable giving: A multivariate analysis. *Voluntas: International Journal of Voluntary and Non-profit Organizations. 8*, 235-260. doi:10.1007/BF02354199

Schortgen, A. C. (2006). The face of donors in America: Who gives and why it matters. (Doctoral dissertation). Retrieved from ProQuest Digital Dissertations. (AAT No. 3224399)

Scott, G. G. (2010). How to create a motivating environment. *Nonprofit World. 28*(5), 9. Retrieved from http://nonprofitworld.org

Semuels, A. (2010, June 30). Economic fears rise as stimulus ebbs: With the job market still weak, the consumer-driven financial engine could run out of gas. *The Los Angeles Times*, p. 1A.

Shaw, M., & Shaw, P. (2008). Overcoming the college president's Achilles' heel: Fundraising. *Diverse Issues in Higher Education. 25*(19), 21. Retrieved from http://diverseeducation.com

Staurowsky, E., Parkhouse, B., & Sachs, M. (1996). Developing an instrument to measure athletic donor behavior and motivation. *Journal of Sport Management. 10*, 262-277. Retrieved from http://nassm.com

Steinberg, R., & Wilhelm, M. (2003). Tracking giving across generations. *New Directions for Philanthropic Fundraising. 42*, 71–82. doi:10.1002/pf.50

Strode, J. P. (2006). Donor motives to giving to intercollegiate athletics. (Doctoral dissertation). Retrieved from ProQuest Digital Dissertations. (ATT No. 3217403)

Sullivan, D. H. (1985). Simultaneous determination of church contributions and church attendance. *Economic Inquiry. 23*, 309-320. doi:10.1111/j.1465-7295.1985.tb01767.x

Tate, E. D., & Miller, G. R. (1971). Differences in value systems of persons with varying religious orientations. *Journal for the Scientific Study of Religion. 10*, 357-365. doi:10.2307/1384781

Teraji, S. (2009). The economics of possible selves. *Journal of Socio-Economics. 38*, 45. doi:10.1016/j.socec.2008.10.003

Thralls, R. (2007). Primer on philanthropic giving. *The Officer. 83*(4), 59. Retrieved from http://roa.org

Valentinov, V. (2008). The economics of nonprofit organization: In search of an integrative theory. *Journal of Economic Issues. 62*, 745-762.

Verner, M., Hecht, J., & Fansler, G. (1998). Validating an instrument to assess the motivation of athletics donors. *Journal of Sport Management. 12*, 123-137. Retrieved from http://nassm.com

Waters, R. D. (2007). Advancing relationship management theory: Co-orientation and the nonprofit-donor relationship. (Doctoral Dissertation). Retrieved from ProQuest Digital Dissertations. (AAT No. 3281621)

Weisbord, R. K., & DeScioli, P. (2010). The effects of donor standing on philanthropy: Insights from the psychology of gift-giving. *Gonzaga Law Review. 45*, 225-289. Retrieved from http://www.law.gonzaga.edu

Whitford, D. (2000). The New shape of philanthropy. *Fortune. 141*, 315-316. Retrieved from http://www.fortune.com

Winthrop, J. (1630). A model of Christian charity. In D.C. Hammack (Ed.), *In making the nonprofit sector in the United States: A reader* (20-27). Indianapolis, IN: Indiana University Press.

Wulfson, M. (2001). The ethics of corporate social responsibility and philanthropic ventures. *Journal of Business Ethics, 29*, 135-145. doi:10.1023/A:1006459329221

Yen, S. T. (2002). An econometric analysis of household donations in the USA. *Applied Economics Letters. 9*, 837-841. doi:10.1080/13504850210148189

Yoruk, B. K. (2008). Three essays on the economics of charitable giving: Implications for fundraising and public policy towards the nonprofit sector. (Doctoral dissertation). Retrieved from ProQuest Digital Dissertations. (AAT No. 3327288)

Ziliak, S. T. (2004). Charity, philanthropy, and civility in American history. *The Journal of Economic History. 64*, 273-275. doi:10.1017/S0022050704412704

Zikmund, W., Babin, B.J., Carr, J.C., & Griffin, M. (2009) *Business research methods* (8th ed.). Thousand Oaks, CA: Southwestern College.

CHAPTER 13: APPENDICES

APPENDIX A:

Permission to Use Survey Instrument

----- Original Message ----
From: James Strode
To: Bobby Olszewski
Sent: Saturday, February 21, 2009 12:43:50 PM
Subject: RE: Your Dissertation Survey

Hi Bobby:

Very nice to hear from you. I have no problem with you utilizing the survey we developed for a donor profile. I have attached a pdf with the dissertation in case you do not have it in hand. Hopefully by year's end, this study will be published in the Journal for the Study of Sports and Athletes in Education, so stay tuned.

Let me know if I can be of further assistance.

jps

____

From: Bobby Olszewski
Sent: Friday, February 20, 2009 3:09 PM
To: James Strode
Subject: Your Dissertation Survey

Dr. Strode:

I hope this e-mail finds you well. My name is Bobby Olszewski from Orlando, FL and I am a doctoral student working on my Ph.D. in Business Administration from Northcentral University. I would sincerely appreciate your nominal assistance for a specific aspect of my own dissertation exercise.

I am conducting some early analysis on my dissertation topic analyzing donor motives. I would very much like to use your survey instrument in my research. I am looking to study donor motivations to an actual religion based on your research. I would like to use your survey instrument to send to the worldwide donors of the National Shrine of Mary Queen of the Universe in Orlando, FL. I would like to use your survey to find the motives of donors giving to a national Catholic shrine.

Again, I am very early in my preparation and would like to see if your survey could even be a possibility. I have also attached my resume to give you an understanding of my professional and academic achievements. Thank you again for your consideration and efforts on my behalf.

Sincerely,

Robert M. "Bobby" Olszewski, M.A., M.S.

APPENDIX B:

Permission to Use Basilica Donor Sample

From: Susan Kimmel
To: Bobby Olszewski
Sent: Wednesday, September 2, 2009 2:33:51 PM
Subject: Letter for Northcentral U.

September 2, 2009

Mr. Bobby Olszewski
1130 Copenhagen Way
Winter Garden, FL 34787

Dear Bobby,

The Basilica of the National Shrine of Mary, Queen of the Universe is happy to work with you on your dissertation at Northcentral University. We will be happy to make available some of our donors for use in your quantitative survey.

Sincerely yours in Christ,

Very Rev. Edward J. McCarthy, STL, D.Min.

EJM/sk

APPENDIX C:

Cover Letter and Ethical Assurance to Participants

September 22, 2010

Dear Basilica of the National Shrine of Mary Queen of the Universe Donor:

You have been randomly selected to participate in a survey for the Basilica of Mary Queen of the Universe. This survey is being conducted to serve the Basilica of Mary Queen of the Universe as well as efforts to complete my doctoral dissertation as a student at Northcentral University (NCU).

Because YOU are such an important contributor to the success of the Basilica, Father Edward McCarthy values your opinions and asks that you promptly complete and return the enclosed survey. This survey is simply seeking your opinions on your personal motivations to give to the Basilica as I use your survey response to complete my Ph.D. dissertation as a doctoral student at NCU.

I thank you for taking the time to complete this survey so the Basilica can better serve your needs as well as help me complete my Ph.D. in Business Administration. Your participation in this survey is 100% voluntary, as you can elect not to participate by simply discarding this mailing. If you choose not to participate, this will not affect your relationship or standing with the Basilica of Mary Queen of the Universe in any way. The results will be used to better understand the motivations of donors giving to a charity such as this one. Fr. McCarthy hopes to use the results to help serve you better.

Your survey responses are confidential as there is no way to track your answers or even your actual participation in this survey. Once you return your survey, the results are tabulated and then used in summaries. You will always remain completely anonymous.

Time is very critical in a survey such as this, so I ask that you complete this survey by **October 25, 2010**. Please be sure to carefully ***answer each question completely*** as we truly need your completed survey back before the end of October. This deadline allows us ample time to process the data and allow your collective responses to be heard.

Thank you again for your completely voluntary and most appreciated participation. If you have any questions do not hesitate to contact me (Bobby Olszewski at 321.217.8687 or anytime via e-mail at TheBobbyO@yahoo.com). Thank you for helping me achieve by Ph.D. from Northcentral University while serving the Basilica of the National Shrine of Mary Queen of the Universe!

Sincerely,

Robert "Bobby" Olszewski	Dr. Michael Millstone	Very Rev. Edward J. McCarthy, STL, D.Min.
Ph.D. Doctoral Candidate	NCU Dissertation Chair	Rector - Mary Queen of the Universe
407-230-6600	602-672-8851	407-239-6600
ROlszewski@ncu.edu	MMillstone@NCU.edu	RectorsOffice@MaryQueenoftheUniverse.org

P.S. Thank you for your assistance in completing the following survey so I can earn my doctoral dissertation and serve the Basilica of the National Shrine of Mary Queen of the Universe. Again, please be sure that you complete this survey by **October 25, 2010** and ***answer each question completely.***

153

Quantitative Basilica Survey Instrument

Instructions: We are interested in what motivates you to donate to the Basilica of Mary, Queen of the Universe. Please remember that your responses to the following 24 questions are 100% anonymous. The following statements represent different donor motivations. Please rate the level that you DISAGREE or AGREE with each statement by circling the number that best represents your selection next to each statement.

Strongly Disagree	**Disagree**	**Neutral**	**Agree**	**Strongly Agree**
1	2	3	4	5

I give to the Basilica of Mary, Queen of the Universe because...

1. I wish the basilica to become the most preeminent Basilica in the United States.	1	2	3	4	5
2. By giving I can voice my opinion on the direction of the Basilica.	1	2	3	4	5
3. Giving to the Basilica is the right thing to do.	1	2	3	4	5
4. By giving I gain a feeling of belongingness.	1	2	3	4	5
5. Being a donor allows me to feel connected with other supporters.	1	2	3	4	5
6. My donation aids in creating the finest facilities and programs.	1	2	3	4	5
7. I can help shape the direction of the Basilica.	1	2	3	4	5
8. My gift provides an opportunity to help future visitors.	1	2	3	4	5
9. I enjoy the feeling of being a part of a large group of supporters.	1	2	3	4	5
10. I always pray for Mary's intersession.	1	2	3	4	5
11. It allows me to exert influence on the decision making of the Basilica.	1	2	3	4	5
12. My donation makes me feel I am helping others in need.	1	2	3	4	5
13. I enjoy being associated with other supporters.	1	2	3	4	5
14. My donation lets me be associated with the success of the Basilica.	1	2	3	4	5
15. I receive timely information that is not readily available to the general public.	1	2	3	4	5
16. I am interested in helping religious charities in need.	1	2	3	4	5
17. Being a donor allows me to develop relationships with others.	1	2	3	4	5
18. I feel pride in the success of the operations at the Basilica.	1	2	3	4	5
19. I am very devoted to Mary, the blessed mother of Jesus.	1	2	3	4	5
20. Associating with the basilica brings me closer to others.	1	2	3	4	5
21. I enjoy the income tax benefits.	1	2	3	4	5
22. I have a great personal affection for the Rector and priests at the Basilica.	1	2	3	4	5

23. Please circle your response below when answering the following question.
During my visit to Mary, Queen of the Universe, locating the basilica was:

1- Very Difficult   2- Difficult   3-Neither Easy or Difficult   4-Easy   5- Very Easy

24. What was the amount range of your specific dollar donation to Mary Queen of the Universe in the last 12 months (one year)? Please circle the amount range below:

$1 - $99	$100 - $199	$200 - $299	$300 - $399	$400 or more
1	2	3	4	5

Your responses are 100% anonymous as your responses only represent past history. The 1-5 scale questions and range amounts are part of the scientific survey used to tabulate the data. There are no future expectations placed on you as a donor based on your 100% anonymous survey responses. Thank you so much for participating!

Please complete this survey by <u>October 25, 2010</u> and *answer each question completely*!